Living and Discovering

G

1) Round Granada Alhambra

2) Go uphill towards Alhambra following signs to A. Palace Hotel

3) Go left down Antequerela Baja and take next sharp right to Campo del Principe

4) Cross the square left into Calle Molinos

5) Turn left again under the arch to the Sueve. Huerta de Los Angeles 8.

Headwater holidays - 01606 720033

Editorial Everest would like to thank you for purchasing this book. It has been created by an extensive and complete publishing team made up of photographers, illustrators and authors specialised in the field of tourism, together with our modern cartography department. Everest guarantees that the contents of this work were completely up to date at the time of going to press, and we would like to invite you to send us any information that helps us to improve our publications, so that we may always offer QUALITY TOURISM.

Please send your comments to:
Editorial Everest. Dpto. de Turismo
Apartado 339 – 24080 León (España)
e-mail: turismo@everest.es

Editorial Management: Raquel López Varela

Editorial Coordination: Eva María Fernández

Text: Gabriel García Guardia

Photographs: Jose Manuel Gutiérrez, Georama and Everest File

Layout: José Manuel Núñez

Cover Design and excursion maps: Francisco A. Morais

Street maps and road maps: Montserrat Gual
© Cartografía Everest

Digital image processing: Marcos R. Méndez

Translation: Polaria

No part of this publication may be reproduced, stored in a retrieval system or transmitted, in any form or by any means, electronic, mechanical, photocopying, recording or otherwise, without the prior written permission of the Copyright holder.
All rights reserved, including the rights of sale, renting, loan or any other use of the book.

Editorial Everest guarantees the total updating of the information contained in this work, until the time of publishing and will be grateful for any sort of information given that may help to improve its publications. Please contact:

© EDITORIAL EVEREST, S. A.
Carretera León-Coruña Km 5, León (España)
Apartado 339, 24080
ISBN: 84-241-0442-0
Legal Deposit: LE. 872 - 2003
Printed in Spain

EDITORIAL EVERGRÁFICAS, S. L.
Carretera León-La Coruña, km 5
LEÓN (Spain)

Living and Discovering
Granada

"Among the four elements, Granada chose water. Water leaping, running and resting in the rooms of the Alhambra, the dreamed oasis."

Gabriel García Guardia.

Index

This is Granada — 6

- Definition and description of the city — 6
- Climate — 8
- Best season to visit — 9
- People and customs — 10
- Historic approach — 13
- Current situation — 20
- Architectonic, cultural, economic and urban development — 21

How to get there and get about — 24

- 24 How to get there
- 26 How to get about

Where to stay — 30

- If you are on a business trip — 30
- If you are looking for a romantic place — 32
- If you are on a reduced budget — 33
- If you are a nature lover — 34
- Accommodations in Sierra Nevada — 35

Trips round the city — 36

- 36 The hill of the Alhambra
- 44 The Albaicín and the Sacromonte
- 54 The Centre
- 63 From the Realejo to the river plain
- 69 The northern area of the outskirts
- 75 Natural, scientific and documental itineraries

Where to eat — 76

- Cocktails, cañas, and other drinks — 78
- For mugs and cups — 79
- Our selection of restaurants — 80

Tapas and drinks — 86

- 87 Areas and establishments

Shopping in Granada — 94

- Areas and types of shops — 95

Nightlife — 102

- 102 Culture life and shows
- 106 Drink bars and trendy areas

Festivities in Granada — 110

- Deep rooted customs and traditions — 110
- Fairs and contests — 115

Granada for children — 116

- 116 Gardens for family walks
- 117 Other gardens and small parks
- 118 Playing and learning
- 119 Toys and teaching material
- 119 Hamburger and pizza bars
- 119 Ice-cream parlour
- 120 Attractions and amusements
- 120 Sporting premises
- 120 Cycling, bike rental, routes, etc.
- 120 Sport centres
- 121 Flying and paragliding
- 121 Water and sea sports
- 121 Ski and mountain sports
- 121 Tennis, golf, riding…

Outings in the surrounding areas — 124

- Border Places — 124
- The conquer of Granada — 126
- After the trail of Lorca — 128
- National Park of Sierra de Huétor — 130
- The Sierra Nevada — 131
- Alpujarras — 133
- The high plateau — 134
- The Coast — 136

Granada in a day — 138

Granada in a weekend — 140

Festivities and Events — 142

Index of names — 144

This is Granada

Definition and description of the city

Granada is one of the most attractive cities of the world for tourism. The climax of its richness in monuments is the Alhambra, which is undoubtedly the sign of identity of the city and one of the most visited monuments in Spain. Legends shaped the past of Granada and its Alhambra. These two names evoke heavenly wonders, but also witnessed events that were decisive for the course of history.

Granada was the place chosen by Romans and Iberians to create important centres of population in the Ancient Times. One of them, known as Illiberis, was chosen as Episcopal see and housed the famous Council of Elvira, in the early IV century. This land was also chosen by the disciples of the Apostles, lead by Saint Cecil, to preach Christianity in Europe. This is the reason why he is the patron saint of Granada and his mortal remains are venerated in the Sacromonte. Centuries later, Abd-al-Rahman I also chose the coasts of Granada to disembark, despite he eventually chose Cordova to found his caliphate. One of the administrators of the kingdom, Zawi ibn Ziri, feels

This is Granada

the attraction of Granada and founds the capital city of his kingdom there, in the hill over viewing the union of the Darro and the Genil. Again, Alamar feels attracted by Granada and founds the Nasrid dynasty. Under its kings, and between the XIIIth and the XVth century, Granada, was the capital of the kingdom, grew in splendour and was crowned by the palaces of the Alhambra.

After the surrender in 1492, the Catholic Monarchs chose Granada and its Royal Chapel as their pantheon. The baroque and Renaissance Granada is built during these centuries, a city where the best artists of the time go to work, creating an exceptional collection of temples, altarpieces, images, pictures, etc.

This aesthetic attraction is continued centuries later and Granada is the Spanish city chosen as source of inspiration and quiet haven by travellers, scientists, painters, musicians like Manuel de Falla or Albéniz, poets like Federico García Lorca and many more artists.

But this legacy of richness in monuments and literature that centuries left in Granada, embraces its current vitality, thus denying any misgiving of daydreaming anchored in the past. Its diverse cultural and artistic inheritance and the magic of its gardens join its colourful quarters, its lively streets, the continuous sequence of cultural, ludic and sporting activities, and of course, the famous nightlife impregnating the streets of the city after dusk.

The city of Granada is located in the centre of its province, with the coast less than 50 miles to the South; the Sierra Nevada to the East, creating a background to the city; the plain of the Genil, open to the West and the wavy mountains bordering the capital to the North. This way, the surroundings of Granada multiply its options for the widest variety of tourist demand.

The steady population of Granada is around 285,000 people, placing it as the fourth biggest city in Andalusia, only after Seville, Malaga and Cordova. The inhabited area is located at an average height of

Granada is one of the points of reference for the tourist sector in Spain. Every step is sprinkled with evocative spot.

This is Granada

Seen from the Alhambra, the inhabited area is a mosaic of chiaroscuro volumes in which life flows with special energy.

2.230 feet, in an exceptional area at the foot of the Sierra Nevada, at the very spot where the conglomerates of the hills of the Alhambra and the alluvial area of the valley meet. A few rivers and crags, many of them hidden by the town planning, divide the city in quarters: the hills of Mauror spread into the quarter of El Realejo, near the mouth of the Darro and the Genil; the hill of the Alhambra stands lonely with its characteristic reddish colour, separated of the Sacromonte and the Albaicin by the river Darro. The hinge between these two quarters is the crag going down the Cuesta del Chapiz, a tributary to the Darro. Heading north, there is another hill where the Cartuja is located. Down in the plain, the quarters spread like "grains of a pomegranate": Plaza de Toros (bullring), Encina, Angustias and Chana in the Northwest; Ciudad Jardín, Vergeles and Zaidín, to the South; La Quinta, San Conrado and Bola de Oro, going up the Genil.

Climate

Granada enjoys a Mediterranean climate. Its southern location –to 37° 10' 35'' N latitude and 0° 05' 15'' E longitude– provides it with one of the brightest and most

Yearly averages	
Maximum in the shade	39,5 °C
Minimum	4,4 °C
Max temperature average	22,1 °C
Min temperature average	10,1 °C
Rainy days	173
Yearly sunny hours	2.850
Ozone	5,19%
Average pollution:	
Suspended particles	0,07%
NO_2	0,48%
CE	0,14%

This is Granada

Average climatology for the last decade in Granada				
Quarterly Average	1st. quarter	2nd quarter	3rd quarter	4rd quarter
Average temperatura	8,8 °C	17,1 °C	24 °C	11,3 °C
Total rainfall	80,2 mm	91,1 mm	0,5 mm	113,1 mm
Sunny hours	586	809	1.009	557

pleasant climates in Andalusia. Winters are very rarely harsh. Snowfall is very infrequent in Granada, and shooting the Alhambra covered by a white blanket is an extraordinary event, when it occurs. Springs are very pleasing and the light is radiant and bright. Summer is hot, like in the rest of Andalusia. Nevertheless, at dusk, the air cools down and Granadines go out with the breeze to walk around its streets and take some fresh air, which is excellent for gatherings or even to get to sleep. Autumn is unhurried and only leaves its grey footprint in a few scattered days in which mist falls over the city. Wind very rarely blows in Granada, and rain falls very scarcely.

Best season to visit

Spring visits should be during the Easter holiday. Summer days may be suffocating, unless when walking near the gardens and the fountains. Fresh nights are very nice for walking and chatting in any terrace. If you are fond of music and dance, the best moment is during the International Festival. Autumn sunsets are widely known by its beauty and in this season, there are also street markets of autumn fruits.

In winter, Granada enjoys the ski season and its nightlife becomes more lively due to the university students, especially on weekends. Whenever you plan to visit, especially if you intend to

Any time of the year is a good moment to enjoy the magic and the unique beauty of Granada.

This is Granada

Summer nights hand over the most pleasant moments to enjoy a good dinner and the immortal flamenco.

admire the Alhambra from the Albaicín for a long while, you should calculate the night of full moon. In those days and right after the sunset, the satellite rises behind the Sierra Nevada and goes above the illuminated Nasrid monument, creating a surprising effect.

People and customs

Variety is a prominent aspect of Granada. It is not only that it is located between the mountains and the plain, or that it joins Arab palaces and Christian churches together, or even that it is equally close to the snow and the tropical coast, it is also the contrast of its people, so varied and different. There are university students toiling in their studies, merchants hurrying in their daily coming and going, very active businessmen in the city centre every morning, visitors and tourists coming together in the historic areas. With them, "lifelong" Granadines coexist with foreign students, the age-old inhabitants of the Albaicín share their space with newcomers, the friends of the Granada City Orchestra mix with the fans of the Espárrago Rock.

That is why nobody is a stranger in Granada. Everybody can find friendship and welfare, anyone can fell just like another grain of the fruit the city represents (Granada in Spanish means also pomegranate).

But watch out for one of the most famous features of Granadine people! A trait that may discourage the not well informed or be shocking for the unaware ones: the malafollá. Probably, the best way to know what it is, is not reading the many essays written about it, but suffering it oneself. It can be found here

This is Granada

and there, in shop assistants, waiters, pedestrians, directors or beggars. Normally it is rather fleeting than permanent and it must not be taken as contempt, lack of manners, disdain or distrust. It can be noticed in some gestures or in

Travellers will always find a souvenir to take back home, for anywhere is good to market in Granada.

This is Granada

The unique historical environment of the Alhambra and the Generalife is a crucible in which all kind of visitants come together.

In Granada, the contrast of cultures and races is part of the everyday life, impregnating the streets with a cosmopolitan atmosphere.

the tone of the answer. But, as we said before, it is better to go and meet it in person. It is also part of Granada.

Historic approach

There are arguments about whether the "Man of Orce" is the first European hominid. If it was so, the story of men in the province of Granada started one million years ago.

This is Granada

Many rests of the following centuries have been found in the caves of Píñar, Darro, Murciélagos, etc.
Iberians populated almost all the province. Among the artistic findings of this culture, one of the most interesting and remarkable sculptures of the antiquity dating from the middle of the IVth B.C., the Dama de Baza, shines with its own light. The original is in the Archaeological Museum of Madrid and copies can be found in the Museum of Granada and the airport. Phoenicians and other seafaring people inhabited the coast of Granada for centuries. Legends, archaeology and history merge to tell the story of the foundation of Granada. The fact is that Romans named several centres of population in the area. The biggest among them where Florentia, Castilia and Illiberis. The last one was translated into Spanish as Elvira and was a famous town because it was an Episcopal see in the first centuries of Christianity and because an important Council was held there (years 309 to 312).
During the Ancient Times, Visigoths kept the Roman district division of Illiberis, and when the Arabs arrived to the Peninsula (year 711) the name of the district is arabized and becomes Ilbira. The district becomes dependent of the Omeya caliphate of Cordova (VIII-X centuries). This governmental capital coexisted with other ancient population centres: Castilia, Garnata...

The Alhambra is the most representative artistic hub of the legacy left by the Islamic culture in Granada.

After the fall of the Caliphate of Cordova, Al-Andalus (the Muslim territories in the Iberian Peninsula) splits in Kingdoms of Taifas that fight among them. Berbers settle in that area and become independent. They are lead by Zawi ibn Ziri, who belonged to the Tunisian royal lineage from which he obtained the Ziri in his name. The city of Elvira is abandoned (year 1010) and the capital of this ephemeral kingdom is located in an old but better fortified fortress, located near Elvira, in the hill Otero de la Vega very near the confluence of the rivers Genil and Darro and taking part of the Jewish settlement called Garnata. This is the moment (1013) when the name Granada arises in history.

This is Granada

Iberians, Romans, Moors and Christians wandered around the old Granada, and all of them left their indelible traces in every corner of the city.

Ziries were warriors, not very cultured and not skilful in politics at all, so they came to an agreement with Jews for administrative and trade activities. The Jewish family Ibn Nagrela enjoyed the favour and the preference of the kings and obtained the supreme honour of becoming viziers. Those were years of ethnic coexistence and religious tolerance, only stained by a few anti-Semitic riots and the unavoidable court intrigues. During this Ziri time the bases of the kingdom of Granada are set, Malaga and Almeria are conquered, the irrigation infrastructures are built and the silk trade is strengthened.

Like the rest of the Kingdoms of Taifas, the kingdom of Granada has a short life and falls under the Almoravides, that are called (1090) from the north of Africa, almost as mercenaries. Almoravides governors respect the location of the capital. They rule from it between the years 1090 and 1154, somehow repressing the non-Muslim. During the period, Granadine literature flourishes with famous poets. The Almohade period (1154-1232) is also prosperous for Granada, with famous and prolific writers, mystics and prose writers, some of them protected by the governor and benefactor Abu Said. The city is fortified and it gets to have 1,200 towers and 20 gates, according to the legend.
The Almohade kingdom, undermined by the internal fights and the advance of the Reconquest that arrives to the Navas de Tolosa (Jaen) in 1212, suffers a fragmentation in which different nobles take over former districts. With this background, Muhammad ben Yusuf ben Nsar, member of the Banu Ahmar (Alhamar) and

This is Granada

Lord of Arjona, creates the Nasrid Kingdom of Granada in 1237-1238, being the capital the former Ziri city. During the first times, the kingdom comprises the modern provinces of Almeria, Granada, Jaen and Malaga, even arriving to Gibraltar, but eventually, it will lose territories and gain in culture and refinement. During this Nasrid period (1238-1492), that lasted for more than two and a half centuries, creation is combined with a look into the past. All the inherited literature is compiled and classified, while science, agriculture and philosophy. The way of life of the caliphs of Cordova is recreated, with the added boost of the thriving trade, arts and craftsmanship.

The dynasty starts with Muhammad I (1237-1273) and ends with Muhammad XII Abu 'Abd Allah, known as Boabdil. The greatest splendour was achieved during the reign of Yusuf and Muhammad V. It was then when the most artistic core of Alhambra and the Generalife is built, the university of La Madraza gains fame in other kingdoms, travellers from all the Islam come to visit Granada and the trade relations with all the Mediterranean region are extensive.

The appearance of Granada changes gradually: with the fall of Baeza refugees from that town move to the Albaicin –which was the origin of its name al-bayazzin, "place of the people from Baeza"–, new quarters are built outside the city walls. Walls that were never used because Granada was never besieged.

The last period is full of internal fights for power. The Zegries and Abencerrajes families conspire against the kings. Muley Hasan (Mulhacen) is married to Aisha

The Alhambra, with its beautiful spots, like the Puerta del Vino, *embraced stories like that of* Boabdil *and* Zorayda.

This is Granada

Dozens of temples were built during the reconquest of the city.

in order to clam animosities down, but the queen retires to Dalahorra with her son Muhammad XII Boabdil, while the king receives Doña Isabel de Solís (Zorayda) in the Alhambra and there they live the last days of their love. Muhammad XII ascends the throne, but he is forced to deliver the city to the Catholic Monarchs, who crown the Reconquest on February 2 of 1492 with the conquer of Granada, after 11 years of victories.
After the expulsion of Arabs and Jews from Granada, the city begins to transform into a Christian symbol. The Catholic Monarchs chose it as their pantheon and the city is sprinkled with dozens of temples, some of them were built following the innovative Renaissance and Baroque canons, some other were former mosques transformed by Mudejar architects. Them all were decorated with thousands of sculptures, paintings and religious ornaments. That is the reason why, during the XVIst century, Granada saw a continuous flow of the best architects, painters and sculptors of the time, who left a deep trace in it. This artistic flow will not decline during the following centuries. The building of monuments and palaces is accompanied by the labour of the institutions: the university, created by Charles V in 1526; the

Sword of Boabdil.

The Alcazaba offers splendid views of the city.

Chancellery, that was the second established in Spain; the Archbishopric, that obtained suffrage from Cartagena to Malaga; the militia and the aristocracy, that placed Granada among the main cities of the kingdom. No wonder its symbol (a pomegranate) is displayed in the Spanish Coat-of-Arms, together with the four historical kingdoms. From 1810 to 1812 Granada was occupied by the Napoleon's troops that savagely ransacked it, destroying many artworks. Years later some quite different French people headed the arrival of Romantic travellers, writers and artists who created in Granada a legend that would be immortalised beyond the Spanish borders. This imaginary Granada, with concealed beauties in the faces of Arab women, shown here and there in the pictures, and hidden treasures under ruins that are nothing but evocation, attracted new visitors and it could be said that is still present in the minds of many modern tourists. All this legend and evocation is backed by real amazing landscapes, unwontedly beautiful and fleeting sunsets, and unforgettable views, sometimes of blinding-white lime, sometimes of surprising green effects, sometimes of mesmerizing mirrors in the water of the fountains.

By the end of the XIXth century, Granada begun to be

The French troops depleted the artistic heritage of the city.

This is Granada

Last years, Granada has grown in modernity, thus increasing its international recognition.

aware of these natural gifts and warily started its launching as a tourist centre. These were years of industrial expansion and there was an economic take off, instigated by the sugar industry. New roads and streets were built, while uninhabitable old quarters were destroyed by the new emerging bourgeoisie. Modernism influenced the new façades of the Gran Vía and, with the arrival of the new century,

Culture oozes from every spot in Granada.

trams came into stage: there was even one to the Sierra Nevada.
Culture thrived during those decades. Ángel Ganivet left his literary legacy to young writers. Manuel de Falla moved to Granada, the most relevant sectors of poetry and theatre united around García Lorca. After the post-war period, Granada joined the economic take off of the nineteen seventies promoted by tourism. The Granadine offer was not only based on creative and smart advertising, but also in the adaptation and construction of tourist infrastructures to receive and satisfy the visitors. Industrial parks, dams to provide de city with water and energy, and even recreation areas for the population started to appear around the city.
As a consequence of those years of prosperity, quarters and streets grown uncontrolled. Occasionally, the pickaxe loots theatres, some Modernist houses in the Gran Via, etc. Some other

HISTORICAL CHRONOLOGY OF GRANADA
Some of the most significant historical dates for Granada are listed.

IV c. B. C.:	First half of the century: Dama de Baza.
309 a 312:	Council of Elvira.
1013:	The Ziri dynasty creates the kingdom of Granada.
1238:	Muhammad Ben Alhamar, Lord of Arjona, creates the Nazari kingdom.
1350-1391:	The Generalife and the central Alhambra are built.
1480-1491:	The Christians reconquer Alhama, Loja, Baza...
1491:	Columbus visits the Royal Camp in Santa Fe. This moments represented in a sculpture of M. Benlliure located in the square of *Isabel la Católica* (Isabella the Catholic), in the city centre.
1492:	The Catholic Monarchs receive the keys of the city from the last king: Abu Abdullah, known as *Boabdil el Chico* (the little) in Spanish.
1505:	The chancellery is created. Start of the works of the Royal Chapel, built to house the mortal remains of the Catholic Monarchs and their descendents.
1523:	The Cathedral works start on the site of the old mosque.
1526:	Emperor Charles V resides in the Alhambra. His Palace is built and the University is founded.
1550:	Saint John of God dies in Granada, leaving a reputation as a saint.
1572:	*Moriscos* (moors converted to Christianity) rebel in the Albaicín and the Alpujarra, Ben Humeya being the leading chieftain. John of Austria suppresses the rebellion.
1666:	Alonso Cano works in the tower and the front of the Cathedral.
1650-1790:	Flourishing of the Granadine school of *imaginería* (the carving and painting of religious icons). José de Mora carves its Christ in the Albaicín.
1704:	The Cathedral is finished.
1808-1812:	Granada is occupied by Napoleon's troops.
1840:	Javier de Burgos, born in Motril and current Minister of Public Works, proposes the division of Spain into provinces: The former kingdom of Granada is distributed among the provinces of Granada, Jaen, Malaga and Almeria.
1898:	Federico García Lorca is born and Ganivet dies.
1900:	The Gran Via is built.
1920:	Manuel de Falla moves to Granada.
1936-1939:	Civil War Many people from Granada are murdered during the first days. The poet García Lorca and the Bishop Guadix were among the dozens killed.
1965-1980:	Economic take off. Inauguration of the airport.

The development of Granada is done respecting the surrounding natural spaces.

times, inharmonious glass and concrete parallelepipeds come out.
After the transition of the nineteen seventies and eighties, Granada combined its touristy renovation with a great cultural atmosphere. Despite the reduction of the university district, the University remains one of the essential driving forces of the city. The autonomic administration moved a few services to Granada, like the High Court of Justice, the Library of Andalusia or the Centre of Musical Documentation, which rounded off the important administrative side of the city. Granadine poets, novelists and musicians receive manifold national and international recognitions, measuring the general zeal to modernize the city in order to face the new century, that will make of this a set to be watched and heard.

Current situation: development, importance, problems and most outstanding achievements

Granada is still one of the main cities in Spain. Its importance as a tourist centre is added to the development of its services, its dynamic projects, a great influence in neighbouring regions and an immense attractive as a residential area. Its university

The numerous magic spots and the university life permeate the city with a generational optimism.

This is Granada

has a significant number of faculties and its professionals benefit from a well-earned excellent reputation. Businesses are wealthy and varied. The number of telephone lines is over one hundred thousand. Despite there is only one local newspaper (Ideal), there are several local TV stations, a spacious Congress Centre and an obvious determination to continually modernise the existing infrastructures. Coordinating the road traffic in a city that is definitely not designed for it is hard in any historical locality, but the case of the Granadine Albaicín is even more complicated because of its particular relief and its Islamic planning. Road communications have been significantly improved and the efforts are now focused in enhancing the communication with the coast, the railroad and the airport.
The conservancy of a vast historical, artistic and urban legacy, together with the task of adapting it to be lived in present, rebuilding and

The old Arab city gave way to wide avenues, making a modern, bright, tourist and dynamic city of Granada.

rehabilitating it with respect and art is not an easy job. The Granada of the XXIst century aspires to creatively achieve that point of environmental balance proposed in the postulates of modern creation, especially in the river plain and the agricultural and wild areas surrounding the city that must be preserved.

Architectonic, cultural, economic and urban development

The centre of Granada is built on the site of a former Arab city. Therefore, the town planning is labyrinthine and, in many cases, opening it to the road traffic is impossible. Lustrums in which plans were made for demolishing the old town to build wide avenues, like Gran Vía de Colón, gave way to times full of town

This is Granada

Plaza de la Universidad (University Square). The campus generates important revenues for the city.

planning insanity that, for instance, originated the Camino de Ronda. By the end of the XIXth century, the route of the river Darro across the city (Plaza Nueva, Reyes Católicos, Puerta Real and Acera de Darro streets) was covered in order to allow road traffic to the city centre, and by the end of the XXth century, the Genil has been channelled. Due to historical reasons, the city of Granada is poor in residential areas with mansions and small palaces, and is broken up in new architecturally humble quarters (Zaidín, Chana, Almanjáyar…) Due to the presence of the hills in the east, real state interests are focused on the south and the west, where the agricultural wealth of Granada is.

Granadine economy is very focused on a few areas, tourism and small businesses being most important. On the contrary, it lacks a sound industrial infrastructure, the deep-rooted agriculture is still relevant and the companies are mainly small or medium-sized. Among them, the most relevant in the Autonomous Community manufacture

The channelling of the river Genil has been the last hydraulic work done in Granada in the end of the XXth century.

This is Granada

building materials, paving materials and food. Granada has an important administrative soundness. The Court, the University and the different delegations of the Junta de Andalucía (Autonomic Government) round off a wide payroll that generates a sustained consumption.

Today, Granada is a bright, business and touristy city committed to modernity and one of the most dynamic and youthful in Spain. Its nights and nightlife are famous even beyond the Spanish borders. This is why Granada has so much to live and show. As well as unique buildings, the superabundant artistic inheritance and cultural references of all kinds, the visitor is offered with a view from the balcony of the genuine Mediterranean way of life, free from artifices and a excessively "Andalusian" pose, with a cosmopolitan liveliness, but with the quality of life of a small city. Granada is one of the most affordable cities of Spain, with modernized services and a proverbial hospitality that unite to make the stay of every visitor most pleasant, in a harmonious coexistence with its people.

The streets of the city are full of items that will keep your memories alive.

Small businesses put a colourful touch in the streets of Granada.

How to get there and get about

Granada, a travel in time itself, is a conglomeration of cosy spots and avenues. Past, present and a promising future enhance the balance that has been attained between the old museum-town and the modern and active capital, where the cameras of the tourists flash everywhere, trying to capture snippets of history. Its enviable tourist attractions are ensured by its location in Southern Spain, the good road communications –especially along the coastline– and the closeness of stunningly beautiful natural resources.

HOW TO GET THERE

• Flying
There are three flights from Madrid and three more from Barcelona on working days. The number is reduced to two from each city on Saturdays.

GRANADA AIRPORT
Ctra. Málaga, s/n.
✆ *958 245 200*

IBERIA
Plaza Isabel la Católica, 2.
National reservations:
✆ *901 333 111.*
International reservations:
✆ *901 333 222.*
More information:
✆ *958 227 592*

How to get there and get about

BUS SERVICE
GRANADA-AIRPORT
Departure from the Congress Centre (front entrance). Paseo del Violón, s/n.
✆ 958 278 677 / 958 131 309

• Railway
RAILWAY STATION
Avda. Andalucía, s/n. ✆ *958 271 272.*

TRAVELLER SERVICE OFFICE
✆ 958 204 000

• By road
Bus station:
Carretera de Jaén, s/n.
✆ 958 185 010

ALSINA - GRAELLS
Bus station:
✆ 958 185 010.
(Seville, Malaga, Almeria, Alpujarra and other southern destinations.)

BONAL
Granada Bus Service - Sierra Nevada:
P.° del Violón (with Puente de la Virgen, Ventorrillo bar).
✆ 958 811 106 / 958 273 100.
Direct service with daily departures at 9h. Also to the eastern villages: Monachil, Huétor, etc.

AUTEDIA
Rector Marín Ocete, 10.
✆ 958 280 592.
Buses to the NE of the province: Guadix, Baza, etc.

BACOMA
Carretera de Jaén, s/n.
✆ 958 157 557

COACH GRANADA - MADRID
Bus station
Direct service between both cities. Two stops in Madrid: South station and Alenza street Coaches almost every hout. Travel length: 5 hours.

There are many Ganadine travel agents, as well as branches of the most important at a national level. They are located in the city centre and most of them sell bus, train or plain tickets.

ENATCAR
Puerta Real, s/n. ✆ *958 284 251*

IBERBÚS
✆ 958 270 189

Tourists arriving to a city hotel.

How to get there and get about

Distances to other Spanish capitals of province (in kilometres):

Almería	166 km
Barcelona	868 km
Bilbao	829 km
Cádiz	335 km
Córdoba	165 km
Huelva	350 km
Jaén	99 km
Madrid	433 km
Málaga	127 km
Murcia	278 km
Sevilla	256 km
Valencia	519 km
Zaragoza	725 km

Distances to other towns in the province of Granada (in kilometres):

Alhama de Granada	59 km
Almuñécar	97 km
Baza	106 km
Guadix	59 km
Huéscar	158 km
Lanjarón	48 km
Loja	58 km
Motril	74 km
Órgiva	58 km
Sierra Nevada (Ski station and Paradores)	44 km
Ugíjar	113 km

The best way to get to know the city is walking around it. No hurries!

JULIÁ
Avda. Andalucía, s/n. ✆ 958 276 766

JINE BUS
Avda. Andalucía, s/n. ✆ 958 276 757

NEVAMAR BUS
Avda. Andalucía, 7. ✆ 958 290 958

HOW TO GET ABOUT

• **City bus**
The company Rober (information: ✆ 900 710 900) has more than 20 lines in Granada. The most popular ones (number 1, 4 and 8) cross the city from north to south.
There are also univerity lines going to the faculties. Lines 10 and 3 connect with the bus station and most of them pass near the train station. The microbuses identified by the words "Alhambra bus"

How to get there and get about

take to the Alhambra, the Albaicín and even connect both hills, every few minutes. Take them at the Plaza Nueva. The ticket price is 1 €, but there are discount tickets for frequent riders.

• Taxis

RADIO-TAXI
℘ 958 151 461

TELE-TAXI
℘ 958 280 654

TAXI UNION
℘ 958 271 075

• Rent-a-car

ALQUIAUTO
Cristo de Medinaceli, 1.
℘ 958 255 747

ATASA
Plaza Cuchilleros, 1.
℘ 958 224 004

ATESA
Molinos, 66.
℘ 958 227 815

AUTOS FORTUNA
Recogidas, 36.
℘ 958 260 254

AUTOS GUDELVA
Pedro Antonio de Alarcón, 18.
℘ 958 251 435

AVIS
Recogidas, 31. ℘ 958 252 358

BUDGET
Recogidas, 35. ℘ 958 250 554

EUROPSAR
Avda. del Sur, 12. ℘ 958 295 065

HERTZ
Luis Braille, 7. ℘ 958 252 419

ITAL
Plaza Cuchilleros, 12.
℘ 958 223 524

• Other vehicle rental

MANOLO MAXI BICICLES
Manuel de Falla, 12.
℘ 958 252 714

AUTOCARES APYME (COACHES)
Fray Leopoldo Alpadeire, 9.
℘ 958 290 311

CARAVANAS CARDONA (CARAVANS)
Callejón del Ángel, 7.
℘ 958 819 555

The surroundings of the Alhambra.

How to get there and get about

Tourists taking a bus.

Coches de lujo, especiales y todo terreno Fortuna (luxury, special and off-road cars)
Camino Purchil, 2.
℘ 958 260 254

Jet skis and devices for water sports, scuba diving, etc. can be rented in the coaster localities. In the Sierra Nevada, renting equipments for adventure and snow sports is possible.

• **Public car parks**
Public car parks in Granada very rarely come to a standstill. Those in the city centre are in Puerta Real, Mercado de San Agustín, etc. The best option is leaving the vehicle in a car park and walk around the city centre, as its planning, inherited from a historical past, is not favourable for driving, let alone parking. There is a large public car park at the Alhambra, but public transport is more comfortable and affordable.

The city has a significant number of taxis.

USEFUL ADDRESSES AND TELEPHONE NUMBERS

Information offices
Tourism Office of the Junta de Andalucía (Autonomic Government).
Corral del Carbón, Mariana Pineda, s/n. ✆ 958 225 990 / 958 221 022
Tourism Office of the City Council
Pl. Mariana Pineda, 10-bajo.
✆ 958 226 688 / 958 223 528
Provincial Trust for Tourism (Patronato Provincial de Turismo).
Mariana Pineda Square, 10-2.º
✆ 958 223 527

Tourism Guides
Service of Tourism Interpreters/Guides.
Next to Alhambra box offices.
✆ 958 229 936
Rafael Rodríguez.
Santiesteban Márquez, 4.
✆ 958 281 741

Communication services
Postcode 18.000
There are booths in the city centre and near the monuments. No public telephone booth available.
Telephone information: 1003
Mail service, telegraph, fax, etc.
Puerta Real, s/n. ✆ 958 224 835/ 902 197 197
Telephone telegrams.
✆ 958 222 000 / 958 222 008
Information on roads and traffic.
Breakdown service.
✆ 900 123 505 / 917 421 213
Tele-ruta (telephonic service to find the best route).
✆ 915 352 222
Civil Guard of Road Traffic.
✆ 958 153 600
Citizen information.
✆ 900 509 292

In case of emergency:
Granada city council.
Carmen Square, 5. ✆ 958 248 126
Lost and found.
Carmen Square, 5. ✆ 958 248 103
Local Police.
Emergencies. ✆ 092
Carmen Square, 5. ✆ 958 209 461
National Police.
Emergencies. ✆ 091
Regional police station: Duquesa, 15.
✆ 958 278 300
Guardia Civil.
Emergencies. ✆ 062
Central Quarter: Avda. Pulianas, Pol. Almanjáyar, s/n. ✆ 958 251 100
Civil Defence Organization.
Government's subdelegation.
✆ 958 278 650

Healthcare
Health emergencies. ✆ 061
Hospital of the Andalusian Healthcare Service. Avda. Constitución, 100. ✆ 958 241 100/ 958 241 101
San Juan de Dios Hospital.
San Juan de Dios, 15. ✆ 958 275 700/ 958 204 300 / 958 241 100
Hospital Clínico Universitario San Cecilio. Avda. Dr. Olóriz, 16.
✆ 958 275 900 / 958 270 200
Red Cross. ✆ 958 222 024
Ambulances. ✆ 958 282 000
Alhambra Ambulances.
✆ 958 426 320
Information on duty chemists.
✆ 958 271 717
24 h chemist. Recogidas Street, 50.
Fire brigade.
✆ 080/ 958 163 222/ 958 163 211/ 958 160 878
Office of Information to consumers and users.
Gran Capitán, 22. ✆ 958 294 700

Where to stay

Granada has a very wide offer in accommodation. There are big hotels, together with smaller establishments "with charm", affordable guesthouses, campsites and houses where young travellers, adventurers or students usually stay. The services offered depend on the category, but are normally careful and under the close supervision and control of the tourist authority, to which the requests for information and complains must be addressed.

Reservations in Granada:
✆ 958 135 814

Hotels in Granada: *www.spa.es/ turismo/ spain/granada/hotel.htm*

Where to stay on business trips

H**** CARMEN
Acera del Darro, 62.
✆ *958 258 300*
FAX *958 256 462.*
e-mail: hcarmen@jet.es
 *283.* ♣♣♣

It is a dynamic establishment, located at the heart of the city centre. It is a very suitable place for business and social meetings. Well-equipped rooms in comfortable high-standing premises with a marble-based decoration. Private halls and conference rooms. Car park, swimming pool and other services.

Where to stay

H**** Granada Center
Avda. Fuente Nueva, s/n.
✆ *958 205 000.* FAX *958 289 696.*
🛏 *171.* ♣♣♣

Located in a recently constructed building, with attention to details and comfort, and very complete decoration and services. Car park and easy access from the dual carriageway. Comfortable conference halls. Located in front of the Faculty of Science.

H**** Luz Granada
Avda. Constitución, 18. ✆ *958 204 061.*
FAX *958 293 150. www.hoteles-ma.es*
🛏 *175.* ♣♣

Once, it was the most modern hotel in Granada. After a comprehensive renovation, it has re-opened with new services and a good atmosphere. Very bright rooms. Wide range of regular services. A stone throw away from the train station. Easy access by car.

H**** Meliá Granada
Ganivet, 7. ✆ *958 227 400.*
FAX *958 227 403.*
e-mail: melia.granada@solmelia.es
🛏 *197.* ♣♣

The traditional quality offered by this chain of hotels, in the city centre, very close to the City Hall. Frequent art expositions and antique auctions. Boutiques in the ground floor.

H**** Rallye
Paseo de Ronda, 10.
✆ *958 272 800.* FAX *958 272 862.*
e-mail: rallye@mx.2redestb.es
🛏 *79.* ♣♣

Spacious halls for meetings. Despite it is not very central for sightseeing, it is located in one of the main business areas of the city.

H**** San Antón
San Antón, 74. ✆ *958 520 100.*
FAX *958 521 982.*
e-mail: santon@autovia.com
🛏 *189.* ♣♣♣

It is a modern establishment with a nice marble-based decoration and good services for businesspersons. It is a stone throw away from the Congress

Reception at the Carmen Hotel, located at the very centre and one of the better equipped in Granada.

Where to stay

The environment of the Parador (state-run luxury hotel) of San Francisco, perfectly integrated with the unique background of the Alhambra, is brimming with romanticism and evocation.

Centre. Excellent terrace outside for breakfast in winter and dinner in summer.

H**** SARAY
Tierno Galván, 4. ✆ 958 130 009.
FAX 958 129 161.
e-mail: hotelsaray@h-santos.es
🛏 214. ♣♣♣

Car park, swimming pool and other services. Easy access from the dual carriageway. Located near the Congress Centre. Peace and comfort both in rooms and halls.

H**** TRYP ALBAYZÍN
Carrera del Genil, 46-48.
✆ 958 220 002. FAX 958 220 181.
e-mail: tryp.albayzin@hoyeles-tryp.com   🛏 108. ♣♣

Located in the quiet area of the centre, near the basilica of the Virgen de las Angustias. Traditional Granadine decoration. Large rooms and busy halls.

Where to stay
if you are looking for a romantic place

H***** PALACIO DE SANTA PAULA
Gran Vía de Colón, 31.
✆ 958 805 740. FAX 958 805 741.
e-mail: psantapaula@ac-hotels.com
🛏 75. ♣♣

Luxurious and comfortable hotel, located in the old quarter. The cloister of the former convent of Saint Clair (Santa Clara) has been kept intact after a careful refurbishment.

H**** ALHAMBRA PALACE
Peña Partida, 2.
✆ 958 221 468. FAX 958 226 404.
www.euroflat.es/alhambrapalace
🛏 136. ♣♣♣

The most traditional and antique hotel in Granada. It was built by the Duque de San Pedro, emulating his castle in Láchar. Excellent views over the town.

H**** PARADOR SAN FRANCISCO
Real de la Alhambra (Alhambra).
✆ 958 221 440. FAX 958 222 264.
e-mail: granada@parador.es
🛏 38. ♣♣♣

Where to stay

A charming place in the middle of the Alhambra. The premises keep some of the flavour of the former Franciscan monastery that was transformed into a parador. Excellent terrace for dinning al fresco in front of the Generalife.

H*** Palacio de Santa Inés
Cuesta de Santa Inés, 9 (Albaicín).
✆ *958 222 362.* FAX *958 222 465.*
e-mail: sinespal@teleline.es
🛏 *13 (suites included).* ♣♣♣

Peaceful hotel in a stately home of the XVIth century, at the lower Albaicín. It has a beautiful patio, wooden balconies and galleries with views to the Alhambra.

H*** Washington Irving
Paseo del Generalife (Alixares), 2.
✆ *958 227 550.*
FAX *958 227 559.*
🛏 *42.* ♣♣♣

Located next to the Carmen de los Mártires, where once lived Saint John of the Cross. Its premises have the flavour of the classical hotels of yesterday, with some English notes. It is named after the famous American traveller that once stayed very near.

A1 Cuevas El Abanico
Vereda de Enmedio, 89 (Sacromonte).
✆ *958 226 199.* ♣♣

Typical caves of the Sacromonte, converted into apartments.

Where to stay on a reduced budget

H*** Aben Humeya
Avda. Madrid, 10.
✆ *958 295 061.* FAX *958 271 084.*
🛏 *171.* ♣

Simple and well conditioned. It is very close to the train station and the Faculties of Science and Medicine. Very popular among visiting professors.

H*** Los Ángeles
Cuesta Escoriaza, 17.
✆ *958 221 424.* FAX *958 222 125.*
🛏 *100.* ♣

Despite it is a bit far from the centre, it is perfect for relaxing in its gardens and premises. Comfort and individual balconies over the swimming pool in every room. Car park.

H** Los Jerónimos
Gran Capitán, 1.
✆ *958 294 461.* FAX *958 294 461.*
🛏 *30.* ♣♣

Located in front of the Monastery of San Jerónimo. Despite being so close to the nightlife area, it is a quiet and convenient place.

H** Maciá
Plaza Nueva, 4.

> *The Alhambra, with all its gardens and spots, like the Puerta del Vino (gate of wine), is the perfect scenery to remember unforgettable moments.*

Where to stay

☎ 958 227 536. FAX 958 227 533.
🛏 40. ♣

Located almost at the foot of the Alhambra. The commotion of the square is almost inaudible on the rooms Some difficulties to arrive by car.

H* Molinos
Molinos, 12.
☎ 958 227 489. FAX 958 227 367.
🛏 9. ♣ ♣

Simple house, well decorated, comfortable and a stone throw away from the centre. It has a car park.

H* Niza
Navas, 16.
☎ 958 225 430. FAX 958 225 427.
🛏 19. ♣

Affordable and central. Special offers for groups. Some difficulties to arrive by car.

Many excellent accommodations, like the Cortijo Los Avellanos, can be found in the surroundings of Granada.

Where to stay
if you are a nature lover

H***** La Bobadilla
Finca La Bobadilla. Detour old road Seville-Loja (50 km –31 miles– from Granada).
☎ 958 321 861. FAX 958 225 427.
e-mail: info@la-bobadilla.com

Former Andalusian cortijo transformed into a super luxurious hotel, with all the services, riding school, heated swimming pool, organized hunting, etc. It has a good restaurant, an excellent wine cellar, a chapel with and organ, etc.

CAMPSITES
Sierra Nevada 1st C.
Avda. de Madrid, 107 (Dual carriageway exit 126).
☎ 958 150 062.
✕ *From November 1 to the February 30.*

The closest campsite to the city, well communicated via city bus and very close to the bus station.

Cortijo Los Avellanos de Sierra Nevada 1st C.
Ctra. de La Fábrica, s/n (Dílar).
FAX *958 596 016.*
e-mail: avellana@teleline.es
It is 12 miles far from Granada, by the river Dílar. Installed inside a former cortijo, the cosy infrastructure and a especially inspiring natural environment, make this campsite a perfect place for resting in contact with nature.

Los Álamos 2nd C.
Dual carriageway A-92, km 438 (5 km from Granada). ☎ 958 208 479.
Quiet atmosphere and good premises, adequate for its category.

Cubillas 2nd C.
Cubillas dam, Albolote, old N-323 road, km 117 (some 15 km from Granada). ☎ 958 453 265. ✶ Never.
Good premises and location under a large pinewood, a stone throw away from the water. Perfect for water sport lovers. There are no villages nearby, but buses to Granada pass frequently.

María Eugenia 2nd C.
Dual carriageway A-92, km 438. ☎ 958 200 606. ✶ Never.
Installed in the Vega de Granada. It enjoys an excellent summer weather. Well communicated with rural and outskirt quarters of Granada, like La Bobadilla, and with Macarena and Santa Fe.

Reina Isabel 2nd C.
La Zubia, Ronda Sur, heading the Sierra Nevada (exit 3). ☎ 958 591 191.
The closest campsite to Sierra Nevada, located in the village of La Zubia. Regular bus service to Granada.

Suspiro del Moro 2nd C.
Dual carriageway A-323, km 145. ☎ 958 555 411. ✶ Never.
Located in a quiet place, with good views towards the river plain and Granada.

Horse riding in the Sierra Nevada.

ACCOMMODATIONS IN SIERRA NEVADA

Staying in the Sierra Nevada has an undeniable appeal: no city commotion, very pleasing temperatures in summer, snow in winter, sports, etc. There are several 4-star hotels in Pradollano (Sierra Nevada). Among them, we recommend:

Kenia Nevada
Pradollano, s/n. ☎ 958 480 911

Maribel
Pradollano, s/n. ☎ 958 480 600

Meliá Sierra Nevada
Pradollano, s/n. ☎ 958 480 400

There is also half a dozen of 3-star hotels and some more 2-star and 1-star establishments, as well as apartments, university residences, youth hostels, etc.

Trips
round the city

If you want to get to know Granada well, there are several possible routes or itineraries for walking and sightseeing, according to the topography of the city. They are perfect for those visitors who have the interest but not the time to visit as many Granadine monuments as possible, and want to get an overview of the city through lineal walks.

The start point of every itinerary may be the **Plaza de Isabel la Católica,** which is easy to remember by the magnificent bronze work of the sculptor Mariano Benlliure, located in its centre. It represents Columbus delivering his projects to the Queen Isabel the Catholic at the Real Sitio de Santa Fe. The model was cast in 1892.

ITINERARY I. THE HILL OF THE ALHAMBRA

Start at the above-mentioned Plaza de Isabel la Católica and head to the Plaza Nueva. In front of the Court *(Audiencia)*, there is the stop where buses take visitors to the hill of the Alhambra every five minutes. Walking is also possible, but the way is very steep and strength should be saved for the long sightseeing walk.

Trips round the city

Halfway to the hill, the bus crosses the **Arco or Puerta de las Granadas** (Arch / Gate of the Pomegranates) built in a Florentine Renaissance style for Charles V. This is the entrance to the walled enclosure.

The **Alhambra** is the most famous Arab monument in the world, and the most interesting in Granada. It stands on the top of a reddish soil hill and this colour might be the origin of the name *Alhambra*. Within the walls of this castle-like enclosed fortress, there are military quarters, sumptuous palaces and refined leisure areas. The walled fortress has the shape of a vessel. Its bow, marked by the Torre de la Vela *(tower of the candle)*, as well as its north side are hills looking over the city and the river plain. During the XIIIrd century, Muhammad Ibn Alhamar, founder of the Nasrid dynasty, built the Alcazaba or military citadel (1238) on the site of the rests of Roman and Visigoth constructions. It is located in the west and has numerous towers and trenches. During the following centuries, the works spread to the east until the **Nasrid Royal Palace,** which was later expanded in to the Upper Alhambra, where the rooms of high courtesans and assistants in the palace were placed.

The central Alhambra or Nasrid palaces consists of the *Palacio de Comares* –Comares Palace– and that of the *Leones* –Lions– (XIVth century). The **Palacio de Comares,** built under King Yusuf I, is the most beautiful part of the Alhambra and has two patios (courtyards): the Mexuar, used as court of justice, and the Arrayanes or Comares, not so publicly used. The Room of Mexuar, preceding the namesake

The Alcazaba, a beautiful sample of military architecture of the XIIIth century, emerges above the top of the trees, offering splendid views of the city.

Trips round the city

■ Alhambra and Generalife

Reservations and groups: ✆ 958 220 912.
Box office:
✆ 958 221 503.
Early reservation and purchase fax:
✆ 958 210 584
(at least 7 days in advance and only when tickets are available).
Price per visit: 4.51 €
Tickets are valid for one day only and are sold until one hour before the closing of the premises, as long as the daily maximum has not been met.
☼ Summer (April-September)
Monday to Saturday from 9 to 20 h. Sunday from 9 to 18 h.
Maximum number of daily visitors: 8,400.
☼ Winter (October-March)
Monday to Saturday from 9 to 17:45 h.
Sunday from 9 to 17:45 h.
Maximum number of daily visitors: 6,800.
☾ Night visit.
Tuesday and Thursday from 22 to 24 h. Sunday from 20 to 22 h.

The Patio de los Arrayanes (court of the myrtles), at the Comares Palace, is a spectacle of water and light.

courtyard, was where public hearings were held. On the other side of the Patio Mexuar, there is the *Cuarto Dorado* (Golden Room) with a small milhrab, accessible through a door with a horseshoe arch. The windows of this room, like others in this wing of the palace, open onto the Albaicin, discovering a bunch of white houses alternating with green blots.
The spacious *Patio de los Arrayanes* (Courtyard of the Myrtles) or *Patio de la Alberca* (Courtyard of the Cistern) is the fundamental part of the Palacio de Comares, a perfect harmony of water, green myrtles and plasterwork laboured like

The Patio de los Leones is the most universally known sight of Granada.

The Generalife is a beautiful ensemble of gardens, viewpoints and playful water.

lace. The rectangular pond in the middle, underlined by two myrtle edges, decomposes the towers, battlements, white walls, dark windows and blue sky into iridescent reflections. The small windows hide courtier halls and harem rooms. The Charles V Palace is located in one of the ends. On the other, there is the *Sala de la Barca* (Room of the Boat), with an extraordinary wooden roof, similar to an upturned hull of a vessel. This room gives way to the impressive *Salón del Trono* (Throne Hall) or *Salón de Embajadores* (Ambassadors Hall), which is embedded inside the *Torre de Comares* (Comares Tower) and has a square ground plan, plenty ornaments and elegant, large windows walls are covered with skirting boards of geometric tiling coated with plasterwork.

The Charles V Palace (Palacio de Carlos V) *houses the Museum of the Alhambra.*

The Cuarto de los Leones (Hall of Lions) makes a right angle with the Comares Room and was the private residence of the royal family. The famous *Patio de los Leones* (Lions' Courtyard) is named after the marble fountain in its centre: a twelve-sided basin supported by twelve water spouting lion sculptures. The courtyard has stunning arcades supported by elegant pillars and the decoration is exquisite all around. On one side of this courtyard, there is the *Sala de los Mocárabes* (Hall of the Muqarnas), with coloured stucco and plaster ornaments hanging from the ceiling like stalactites. The *Sala de los Reyes* (Hall of Kings) has rooms with paints in the ceiling. The *Sala de los Abencerrajes* has an interesting ceiling, which is reflected in the central fountain, and the *Sala de las Dos Hermanas* (Room of the Two Sisters), located in front of it, is covered with an impressive Muqarnas dome, and extends to the *Mirador de Daraxa* (Daraxa Balcony). This balcony opens its windows above a peaceful courtyard that gives way to the *Baño Real* (Royal Bath), with rooms embellished with tiles and plasterwork.

By the beginning of the XVIth century Emperor Charles V planned moving to Granada, and the beautiful **Charles V Palace** was built as his residence. The plans of Pedro Machuca were a masterpiece of the Renaissance and a daring composition with a round courtyard inside a square contour.

The Alhambra is completed with several gardens, towers, walls, rooms, Christian temples (Saint Mary, Saint Francis) and superposed buildings.

The **Generalife** is near the Alhambra. It is an ensemble of gardens and small palaces built in the XIVth century and located in the *Cerro del Sol* (Knoll of the Sun), a hill opposed to the Alhambra and the Albaicin. It was the residence of Nasrid monarchs for recreation and retreat, and it consists of terraced gardens, fountains, pools and spouting water and hidden viewpoints from which parts of the Alhambra and the city can be seen. The beautiful palace has two naves and is located in the ends of a large courtyard with a long arcade

Trips round the city

The Charles V Palace guards some of the most interesting artistic inheritances within its walls.

■ **Alhambra Museum**
✆ 958 226 279.
Free entry.
☼ Summer (April-September)
Tuesday to Saturday, from 9:30 to 14:30 h.
☼ Winter (October-March)
Tuesday to Saturday, from 20 to 14:30 h.
Sunday, Monday and holidays, closed.

and a central cistern surrounded by gardens.
The Alhambra and the Generalife have been named a World Heritage Site by UNESCO for its artistic, historical and aesthetic values.
There are two museums inside the Charles V Palace: **Alhambra Museum.** It is located in the ground floor and the access is across the elegant and sober vestibule. In its rooms, there are items from different excavations carried out both in the Alhambra and the other centres of the Arab Granada and its kingdom. Excellent collections of oil lamps, household items, tissues, lamps, Islamic craft items, etc. Ceramics is especially worth mentioning: the articles are many, varied and, generally speaking, well conserved. There are kitchen crockery and decorative items, among which the grand vase of the gazelles has a privileged position. A copy of the sword of Boabdil stands out in the collection of weapons. The original is kept in the Museum of the Army, in Madrid. **Museum of Fine Arts.** It was founded after the *desamortización* (disentailment: confiscation of Spanish Church lands and properties) and the dismantlement of some convents and churches, whose artworks were the first

pieces of the museum's collection. It keeps works from the XVth to the XXth century. Specially relevant are the works of J. Florentino, Alonso Cano, Fray Juan Sánchez Cotán and painters of the school of Granada, like Gómez Moreno, Rodríguez Acosta, Ruiz de Almodóvar, López Mezquita, Juan Cristóbal, Manuel Ángeles Ortiz, etc.

The **Parador de Turismo of San Francisco,** is located inside the historical enclosure of the Alhambra, in a former Franciscan monastery founded by the Catholic Monarchs, on the site of an small Arab palace. The Catholic Monarchs were buried there until 1521, when their mortal remains were taken to the Royal Chapel. Excellent panoramic views and calm in its courtyards. It has been declared a national monument.

Torres Bermejas (Red Towers). Military fortress previous to the construction of the Alhambra and located in the most southern hill. It is one of the oldest military defences of Granada, dated in the VIIIth and IXth centuries.

Carmen of the Rodríguez Acosta Foundation. Interesting *carmen*, built in 1920 by the painter who names it. It has fanciful gardens and keeps paints by foundation grant holders.

■ **Museum of Fine Arts**

Charles V Palace (high floor). ✆ 958 224 843. Free entry for Spaniards and EU citizens. Rest of visitors, 1.50 €
◷ Summer (April-Sept.) Tuesday from 14:30 to 19:45 h.
Wednesday to Saturday from 9 to 19:45 h.
Sunday from 9 to 14h.
◷ Winter (Oct.-March) Tuesday from 10 to 14h.
Wednesday to Saturday from 10 to 14 h. Sunday from 9 to 14 h.
Monday and holidays, closed.

■ **Carmen de la Fundación Rodríguez Acosta**

Callejón Niño del Royo, 8. ✆ 958 227 497

Triptych of the Great Captain, in the Museum of Fine Arts.

Trips round the city

■ **Instituto Gómez Moreno / Fundación Rodríguez Acosta**
Callejón Niño del Rollo, 8. ✆ 958 227 497.
Free entry.
☉ Monday to Friday from 10 to 13:30 h.
Carmen and gardens by previous appointment.

■ **Carmen de los Mártires**
✆ 958 227 953.
Free entry.
☉ Summer (April-Sept.)
Morning from 10 to 14 h
Afternoon from 17 to 19 h. Saturday and Sunday from 10 to 18h.
August closed.
☉ Winter (Oct.- March)
Morning from 10 to 14 h
Afternoon from 17 to 19 h. Saturday and Sunday from 10 to 18 h.

■ **Casa de los Pisa**
Convalecencia, 1.
✆ 958 222 144.
Free entry.
☉ Monday to saturday from 9 to 13h
Afternoons and holidays: previous appointment for groups
Sunday closed.

■ **Archivo Histórico de la Ciudad**
Cuesta del Chapiz, 4.
✆ 958 224 320

■ **El Bañuelo**
✆ 958 222 339.
Free entry
☉ Tuesday to Saturday from 10 to 14 h
Sunday and holidays, closed.

Gómez Moreno Institute. This museum gathers part of the artworks restored and collected by the distinguished Granadine professor and archaeologist Gómez Moreno (1834-1918).

Carmen de los Mártires (Carmen of the martyrs). Beautiful mansion with gardens constructed on the land where once stood a Carmelite monastery that hosted Saint John of the Cross.

Manuel de Falla Centre. Creation of García de Paredes with a splendid auditorium and halls where the program of classical music in Granada is conceived. Here, it meets the fourth itinerary.

ITINERARY II. THE ALBAICIN AND THE SACROMONTE

Its starts at the Plaza Nueva, as well. The **Royal Chancellery** is right there. A beautiful Renaissance-Baroque building of the XVIth century, with an impressive façade, an interesting courtyard with pillars, a lordly staircase and a beautiful Mudejar coffered ceiling. Currently, it houses the Court, so it can be visited from Monday to Friday, in business hours, as long as trials are not interrupted.

The **Casa de los Pisa** is almost behind it. A XVIth century Granadine mansion with a Gothic front and a gorgeous courtyard. Saint John of God, founder of the Brothers Hospitallers, died in this building, which now houses a museum dedicated to the Saint, with paints of Raxis and other.

In front of it, by the other side of the river, there is the **Church of Saint Anne** (first third of the XVIth century), with a graceful Renaissance stone front, a Mudejar tower and one of the best coffered ceilings in Granada. Impressive Lady of Sorrows *(Dolorosa)* by José de Mora.

Following the *Carrera de Darro,* going up the right river bank, there is **El Bañuelo** (the small bath). Arab baths from the XIth century, restored in 1928. They are the most important and comprehensive in Spain.

Trips round the city

In front of them, there are the ruins of the **Puente del Cadí** (Cadí Bridge). It was built in the XIth century and demolished by the middle XVIIth century, it keep a prismatic tower and the start of a splendid horseshoe arch. It once united the Alhambra and the Albaicín.

Go up a passage behind the *Bañuelo,* to arrive to the **Convento de la Concepción.** Founded in the XVIth century, it has an interesting pointed gate and a Baroque interior with sculptures of Pedro and Alonso Mena. It is in front of the **ruins of the Maristán,** an Arab hospital for insane and "innocent" people.

Back to the river bank, we can see the **Convento de Santa Catalina de Zafra** (Convent of Saint Catherine of Zafra). Also dating from the XVIth century, founded by Leonor de Torres and used by Dominican nuns. There is still a small Arab house of the XIth and XIVth centuries inside it. Interesting Renaissance front and Baroque altarpiece. Traditional sweets. The following building is the **Casa de Castril.** It is one of the most beautiful Granadine palaces. Built in the XVIth century, it has a remarkable Renaissance façade: great decorative opulence, full of allegories and mythological symbols. Interesting courtyard and staircase. It currently houses the **Provincial**

In the Plaza Nueva *(New Square), the* Real Chancillería *(Royal Chancellery) unfolds a magnificent Renaissance style in its splendid façade.*

■ **Museo Arqueológico Provincial**
Carrera del Darro, 43.
✆ 958 225 603 /
958 225 640.
Free entry
☉ Summer (April-September)
Tuesday from 15 to 20 h
Wednesday to Saturday from 9 to 20 h
Sunday and holidays, from 9 to 14:30 h
☉ Winter (Oct-March)
Tuesday from 10 to 14 h
Wednesday to Saturday from 10 to 14 h
Sunday and holidays, from 10 to 14 h
Monday closed.

Trips round the city

Archaeological Museum. Interesting and valuable Iberian, Roman, Visigoth and Arab pieces can be found in it. There are also some of the famous glasses of Castril, ancient Fajalauza ceramics and coins minted in Elvira. The palaeontology and ethnography sections are also worth visiting. Opposite to it, there is the **Church of San Pedro and San Pablo** *(Saint Peter and Saint Paul),* standing proud by the river Darro. It has an elegant façade, a beautiful Mudejar coffered ceiling, a valuable Flemish triptych of the Flagellation, a Baroque altarpiece of the XVIIIth century by José de Mora and a carved sculpture of Saint Francis by Pedro de Mena. The procession of the *Cristo del Silencio* (Christ of the Silence) departs from this church on the night of Maundy Thursday, as well as the *Simpecado* (sinless) of the Granadine *hermandad* (religious association) that goes to the Rocío.

Following the street, we get to the **Paseo de los Tristes** (Promenade of the Sad Ones), a name originated in the tradition of saying goodbye to the funerals on their way to the cemetery in that street. It is the perfect place to admire the Alhambra, both in the winter mornings and the summer nights. At the end of the street, there is the **Puente del Rey Chico** (Bridge of the Little King), and, on the opposite bank, there is the way to the **Fuente del Avellano** (Fountain of the Hazel Tree), where Ángel Ganivet used to hold his gatherings. There are beautiful *cármenes* on the hillside, like that of the *Chapiteles,* where one can attend to flamenco music shows.

The *Cuesta del Chapiz* starts at this right bank of the river. At the start, on the right side, there is the **Palacio de los Córdoba** (Córdobas' Palace). Interesting rebuilding with valuable coffered ceilings. It houses the Historic Archive of the City.

In the way up, there is the **Casa del Chapiz** (House of the Chapiz). It is a duet of Morisco mansions of the XVIth century, with a beautiful courtyard and peaceful gardens. Currently, it is the headquarters of the **School of Arab Studies,** founded in 1932 for the investigation of the Muslim culture and its relations with Granada.

Going still a bit up, there are the **Escuelas del Ave María** and the **Seminario de maestros** (Seminary of Masters), the foundation of Andrés Majón, the priest from

Fajalauza tile work.

The Church of San Pedro y San Pablo by the bed of the river Darro.

Trips round the city

Cuesta del Chapiz, *the start of the rise to the Sacromonte.*

The cármenes are among the most typical sights of Granada.

Burgos, which was initially located in the cave *"maestra amiga"* of the Sacromonte, where this distinguished educator used to live (1888). The **Carmen de la Victoria** (*Carmen* of the Victory) has beautiful gardens and belongs to the University of Granada. At the **Peso de la Harina** (Weighing of the Flour), a name given to a small square where flour was weighed, there is the start of the way to the Sacromonte: a quarter positioned on the hillside, by the bank of the river Darro, in a place called **Valparaíso** that has been praised by Arab and Christian poets.

This way goes winging through *cármenes*, crags and caves, many of them still inhabited by gipsies, and some used for the traditional flamenco shows called

Trips round the city

zambras. This former road to Guadix, from which passages and slope streets start, arrives to the *Ermita del Santo Sepulcro* (Hermitage of the Sacred Sepulchre). Further, the former road between Granada and Levante once followed its way.

Walking past an arch, the raise to the **Sacromonte Abbey** starts. This institution was founded during the XVIIth century by the archbishop of Granada, on the site of some caves that are thought to be the catacombs where Saint Cecil –first bishop and Patron Saint of Granada– was tortured, as human remains and writings in lead were found there. All the raise is sprinkled with crossed offered by Granadine devotees to honour the saint. The **Holy Caves** can be visited. The institution consists of a Collegiate Church or Abbey and a School for ecclesiastical canonical studies that has

The Albaicín, World Heritage.

Traditional interior courtyard at the Albaicín.

been active for decades. The **Abbey** has a magnificent church dedicated to The Immaculate, a superb courtyard with pillars, a lordly staircase with a Mudejar coffered ceiling, a library full of ancient books and some other rooms. Since 1928, part of its artworks have been gathered in a museum where works of G. Davis, Raxis, Herrera, Alonso Cano, Risueño and other Baroque painters can be found, as well as portraits of the distinguished patrons and residents of the Sacromonte. The collection is completed with ancient ornaments, sculptures, liturgical jewellery, etc.

Going back by the same way until the *Cuesta del Chapiz,* there is the raise to the other hill, where the Albaicin stands. Ancient and popular quarter that was named a World Heritage Site by the UNESCO

Trips round the city

The Puerta de Elvira *was the main entrance to the Arab Granada in the XIst century.*

■ **Abbey of the Sacromonte**
✆ 958 221 445.
Tickets: 1.50 €
🕐 Mornings from 11 to 13 h
Afternoons from 16 to 18 h
Sunday closed for Mass from 12 to 12:30 h.
Monday, closed.

in 1994. Its labyrinthine streets and its quiet squares keep some Arab flavour. All the charm of the unknown lies in its calm vitality, in its narrow paved passages and the undying perfume of its gardens, and just a stone throw away from the city commotion. The **cármenes** (traditional Granadine houses surrounded by small gardens) terrace on the hill, offering both the beautiful contrast of the green vegetation and the white walls, and stunning views of the Alhambra and the Sierra Nevada. Visiting the **Albaicín,** as web as a must-do, is a real aesthetic and even emotive experience. Many are the worth seeing spots, some of them locked in the labyrinth of lime and cypress, some other open to the Alhambra, the Sacromonte or the Sierra Nevada. Nothing better than discovering them by yourself. At the Albaicin, as well as several Morisco houses, there are a few remarkable monuments and places embedded in the quarter. We have classified them as they show when going down the hill:

San Miguel Hermitage. In the top of the hill. It gives shelter to a popular pilgrimage festival in late September.

Puerta de Fajalauza (Fajalauza Gate). It used to be the entrance to the city by the quarter of potters. Granadine pottery is still manufactured in the area.

Trips round the city

Churches of San Cristóbal and San Bartolomé. These Mudejar style churches were built on the site of former aljamas.
Colegiata del Salvador (Collegiate Church of the Saviour). A XVIth century construction with an elegant front and a beautiful courtyard that belonged to the main mosque of the Albaicin.
Plaza Larga (Long Square). One of the most hectic among those in the Albaicin. The **Cuesta de la Alhacaba** starts on it and finishes near the **Arch of Elvira.** The ancient Arab wall of the **Alcazaba** –dating from the XIth and XIIth centuries– passes by its side. Let us not forget that this was the original construction on the hill and that the Albaicin emerged around it as a suburb, when the refugees from the capture of Baeza arrived. The wall continues until the **Puerta Monaita** (Monaita Gate), one of the oldest (XIth century) and most majestic ones in the city. This old Alcazaba was placed on the site of the main core of the Roman town of Iliberis. Back up at the *Plaza Larga,* it is easy to get to the **Puerta de las Pesas** (Gate of the Weights), another gate communicating the Alcazaba and the Albaicín, but still open to pedestrians.
Saint Nicholas Church and Viewpoint. Built in 1525, it is one of the most distinctive, due to its high belfry, the effect of its roofs and for being Mudejar but whitened. There is a large cistern and an excellent and very busy viewpoint.

Convent of Santa Isabel la Real. Built in Gothic Elizabethan style and founded by Queen Isabel the Catholic in 1501 on the site of a former palace of Moorish monarchs. Beautiful front by Egas, Mudejar tower with tile, atrium with Castilian flavour, cloister and courtyard with gardens, artistic coffered ceiling and altarpiece with Baroque details.
Daralhorra Palace. Small Arab palace dating from the XVth century placed next to *Santa Isabel* Convent. Aisha, mother of Muhammad XII Abu 'Abd Allah, *Boabdil el Chico,* and last king of Granada, once lived there. Beautiful courtyard with a small cistern, rooms and corridors carved in plasterwork and attractive views to the Hill of San Cristóbal.

The church of San Miguel Bajo *stands on the ruins of a former mosque.*

Trips round the city

■ Colegiata de San Salvador
📞 958 278 644.
Entry: 0,60 €
🕑 Summer (April-Sept.)
Morning from 9 to 13 h
Afternoon from 17:30 to 19:30 h
🕑 Winter (Oct-March)
Morning from 10 to 13 h. Afternoon from 16 to 19 h. Sunday, closed.

■ Palacio de Daralhorra
📞 958 223 411.
Free entry
🕑 Monday and Wednesday from 11:30 to 13 h.

The former Arab University is located in the Palacio de la Madraza.

Church of San Miguel Bajo. Dating from the XVIth century, it has an interesting Renaissance façade and important altarpieces. It was built on the site of a mosque and its façade still shows traces of a XIIIth century cistern surrounded by pillars that Arabs took from the Roman city. The church is sited in a small and very lively squared named after it, with terraces outside, a typically Andalusian cross, views of the new area of the city, etc.

Going down the street facing the door of the church, we get to the **Church of Saint Joseph.** Erected in the early XVIth century on the site once taken by the mosque of the *morabitos* or hermits (VIIIth century). Its planning is simple and it has a Mudejar coffered ceiling in the main chapel, an interesting altarpiece and excellent carves of the Granadine school. **Cristo del Silencio de Mora** (Christ of the Silence by Mora). Next to the church, there is still the cistern of the former mosque and the minaret with the added bells; it is the only minaret previous to the Almoravid style in Spain.

The Calderería (quarter of boilermakers) is a very lively area, due both to the daytime trade and the tea establishments

and the nightlife. We walk down to the Elvira street, back to the start point.

ITINERARY III
THE CENTRE

Starting at the *Plaza de Isabel la Católica,* take the *Gran Vía de Colón,* and then the **Zacatín,** the first turning on the left, a famous uphill street named in ballads.

The Royal Chapel was conceived as the final resting place for the Catholic Monarchs.

Halfway up the street, opposite to the *Corral del Carbón,* there is the **Alcaicería:** an ensemble of narrow streets between the river Darro and the former **Mosque,** that once was an Arab silk market and today is a permanent market of

Trips round the city

Trips round the city

Panoramic view of the Cathedral of Granada.

Trips round the city

The cathedral enclosure guards the Pantheon of the Catholic Monarchs, as well as other artistic treasures.

Granadine handicrafts. Next to traditional shops where Castilian handicrafts and works from other Spanish regions are sold, there are also Moorish inspired stalls where leather items and Moroccan articles are sold. Whether you buy or not, it is a very attractive sight for visitors.

Madraza Palace. Built onto the Alcaicería, opposite the Royal Chapel, there is the former **Arab University,** erected in the XIVth century by king Yusuf I. It was one of the noblest edifications of the Muslim Granada. The mirab has been restored. Its main hall has a splendid coffered ceiling. Its façade was later decorated and painted in a

Trips round the city

Baroque style so that it could be used as Town Hall. Currently, it is the Exhibit and Conference Hall of the University of Granada.

Royal Chapel. The Catholic Monarchs commissioned its construction as a pantheon for them and their dynasty in 1504. This Gothic Elizabethan edifice was built according to the plans of Enrique Egas, and has a single nave with a flowery pointed gate that ended up inside the Cathedral. The gate into the street is Plateresque. Especial mention must be made of the central grating (by Bartolomé de Jaén), the peak of the Plateresque forging. Also remarkable are the altarpiece, some valuable Flemish paints and carved sculptures, as well as the mausoleums of the Catholic Monarchs (by Domenico Fancelli) and Phillip the Handsome and his wife Joan the Mad (by Bartolomé Ordóñez). Under these wonderful marble recumbent statues, there is the crypt where the bodies of those four monarchs and the Prince Miguel's are kept in lead coffins. In the XVIth century the mortal remains of the wife of Charles V and the first wife of Philip II were kept there, but were relocated to the Escorial when this king designated it as his pantheon. In the inside, it is communicated with the Cathedral and the Church of the *Sagrario*. The Sacristy, a museum now, has a

■ **Capilla Real**
✆ 958 229 239.
Entry: 1,80 €
☼ Summer (April-Sept.)
Morning from 10 to 13 h
Afternoon from 16 to 19 h
Sunday and holidays,
from 11 to 13 h.
☼ Winter (Oct-March)
Morning from 10:30
to 13 h. Afternoon from
15:30 to 18:30 h
Sunday and holidays,
from 11 to 13 h

■ **Catedral**
✆ 958 222 959.
Entry: 1,80 €
☼ Summer (April-Sept.)
Morning from 10:30
to 13:30 h
Afternoon from 16 to 19 h
Sunday and holidays,
from 16 to 19 h.
☼ Winter (Oct-March)
Morning from 10:30 to
13:30 h. Afternoon from
15:30 to 18:30 h
Sunday and holidays,
from 15:30 to 18:30 h

Missal of the Catholic Monarchs at the Royal Chapel.

Trips round the city

Church of San Justo y Pastor.

priceless collection of Flemish oils on board –especially remarkable is the triptych by D. Bouts– and personal belongings (crown, sceptre, sword, etc.) donated by the monarchs to this chapel.

The **Cathedral** at the *Plaza Pasiegas,* the entrance for tourists at the Gran Vía. It is thought to be the first Renaissance church in Spain. The works started in 1518 on the site of a former mosque, and the architects were, successively, Enrique Egas, Diego de Siloé and Juan de Mena. Despite its Gothic ground plan and Renaissance elevation, there was enough time to finish the Baroque main gate, a masterpiece by Alonso Cano with a rose window by Risueño, in which the Announcement is depicted. The tower though is still unfinished. Remarkable gates: Ecce Hommo, *San Jerónimo* (Saint Jerome) and *el Perdón* (the mercy), the last one being well proportioned, grandiose and decorated with relieves. The bright inside has four naves, ambulatory and elegant pillars with Corinthian semi pillars. In the main chapel, there are the praying statues of the Catholic Monarchs, an altarpiece with the story of the Virgin Mary painted by Cano, magnificent stained glass windows and sculptures by Mena and Medrano. The many chapels have very valuable pieces of art. The ones located at both sides of the main door house the **Cathedral Museum** now, and have important sculpture and paint works, as well as articles worked in precious metals, pieces of jewellery and liturgical ornaments. The Sacristy guards a beautiful Christ and the famous Immaculate Conception by Cano, one of the most precious gems of Spanish art. The Baroque **Church of the Sagrario,** with its Greek cross ground plan, fills the angle created by the Royal Chapel and the Cathedral. Its pillars and vaults resemble the Cathedral, but its style is more Baroque. It has an academic front of grey marble from the Sierra Elvira and abundance of marbles in its tabernacle.

Archbishop's Palace. It is located in front of the **Church of the Sagrario** and has a remarkable collection of paintings of the leading Granadine painters, as well as some of Zurbarán, Lucas Jordán and Ricci. Built onto it, there is the *Curia Eclesiástica* (ecclesiastical curia). The works started in the XVIth century and it was the headquarters of the University of Granada, created by Charles V in 1526. Its well proportioned Plateresque front and its beautiful courtyard with pillars are exceptional. Both buildings are closed to the public due to restoration works. The San Jerónimo Street starts in front of the side of the Cathedral, opposite to the Royal Chapel. In the middle of this street, there is a small square where the **Antiguo Colegio de Jesuitas** (Former Jesuit School) stands. At the moment, it houses the Faculty of Law. It was the *Colegio de San Pablo* (School of Saint Paul) until the expulsion of the Jesuits, in 1767. Since 1769 it was the headquarters of the University. It keeps the front of the XVIIIth century with Solomonic pillars and a sculpture of the Immaculate Conception. The Assembly Hall was the Auditorium, and the study courtyards were the cloisters with arches and Doric pillars of the XVIIth century.

The **church of San Justo y Pastor** is also at the University Square. It is one the most important fruits of the Granadine Baroque. Built in 1575, it was a collegiate church and occupied by the Company of Jesus. It has a beautiful XVIIIth century front in grey and white marble, a remarkable dome and a golden altarpiece decorated by Bocanegra.

■ **Monasterio de San Jerónimo**
C/ Rector López Argüeta, 9. ✆ 958 279 337.
Entry: 1,80 €
☼ Summer (April-September)
Morning from 10 to 13:30 h
Afternoon from 16 to 19:30 h
☼ Winter (Oct-March)
Morning from 10 to 13:30 h
Afternoon from 15 to 18:30 h

The Royal Monastery of San Jerónimo embraces two beautiful interior courtyards.

Trips round the city

Four centuries after its foundation, San Juan de Dios *Hospital keeps rendering the service for which it was created.*

■ **Basílica de San Juan de Dios**
✆ 958 275 700.
☉ Summer (April-September)
Morning from 7:30 to 10:30 h
Afternoon from 18 to 21 h
☉ Winter (Oct-March)
Morning from 7:30 to 12 h
Afternoon from 18:30 to 21 h

Following San Jerónimo Street, we find the **Colegio Mayor San Bartolomé y Santiago** (Hall of residence Saint Bartholomew and Saint James). This foundation of the XVIIIth century established in this palace, a genuine sample of the lordly Granadine constructions of the Baroque. Elegant front in which the house's balcony has been transformed into a niche for exhibiting the saints of the church. Walking a bit further, we come across the **Iglesia del Perpetuo Socorro** (Church of the Perpetual Help), governed now by Padres Redentoristas Order, and walking past *Gran Capitán* Street, there is the **Real Monasterio de San Jerónimo** (Royal Monastery of Saint Jerome). This Renaissance style monument, created by Jacobo Florentino el Indiaco, Diego de Siloé and dozens of other artists, is one of the most significant in Granada. The single-nave church has exquisite classic proportions and its walls were painted during the Baroque period. Wonderful altarpiece by Vázques el Mozo, with sculptures about the life of Jesus and Saint Jerome Penitent. The mortal remains of Gonzálo Fernández de Córdoba, the Great Captain, rest at the feet of the high altar. The coat-of-arms of this soldier and his wife are guarded in this temple, as well as allegories of the virtues in which they are compared with biblical and mythology heroes. The convent, a real piece of art, has two beautiful large courtyards with stone arches and elegant galleries. The biggest of them can be visited. An order of nuns live in the convent and elaborate traditional sweets.

A stone throw away from the convent, there is San Juan de Dios Street, where the **San Juan de Dios Hospital** is. It is the first foundation of the Hospitaller order in Granada. The Portuguese Saint John of God, who arrived to Granada in 1536 and died there in 1550, founded this order, devoted to the care of ill persons. The building, still working as a hospital, has an elegant marble front, a Renaissance coffered ceiling in the vestibule, an impressive courtyard with Baroque tiles and frescos about the life of Saint John, and a particular staircase, with marbles, farsh with ribbon and valuable paintings.

The **basilica of Saint John of God** is next to it. It is the apotheosis of the Granadine Baroque, and was built between 1737 and 1759. The basilica has a rich stone and marble front and its inside is decorated with paintings, sculptures, mirrors, marbles and thousands of golden figurines. In the centre of the altarpiece, a perfect example of Baroque style, there is a small chamber where an urn with the mortal remains of Saint John of God, co-patron saint of Granada, is guarded. Walking around between San Juan de Dios Street and Gran Vía, one can find mansions, convents like **Saint Paula's** (ruined) and houses with Modernist façades. This way, we get back to the Isabel la Católica Square, where the itinerary started.

ITINERARY IV
FROM THE REALEJO TO THE RIVER PLAIN

From the Isabel la Católica square, walk a few blocks down Reyes Católicos Street until the **Corral del Carbón** shows on the left *(Mariana Pineda* Street). This is the oldest monument left by the Arabs in the lower city. It is a very well conserved and unique in Europe warehouse for goods or Arab grain *alhódiga*. It was used as an

The Corral del Carbón *is the only XIVth century fondak still standing in Europe.*

Trips round the city

■ **Casa Museo Manuel de Falla**
Antequeruela Alta, 1.
☏ 958 229 421.
Entry: 1,50 €
☉ Summer (April-September)
Tuesday to Saturday from 9 to 15 h
☉ Winter (Oct-March)
Tuesday to Saturday from 10 to 15:30 h
Sunday, holidays and Monday, closed.

open-air theatre (corral) in the XVIth century, as a hostel for merchants and coal store, an activity to which it owes its name. It has also been a corrala (housing building). Today, it houses the facilities of tourism promotion, handicraft sale and, in some occasions, theatre and flamenco shows. Its wide façade and its elegant courtyard with several sections of balconies are worth mentioning.

Now comes the strolling around the labyrinth of narrow streets sited at the back of this monument. This is how we get to the **quarter of San Matías**, the remains of the former Jewish quarter of Granada that still keep part of its labyrinth of passages.

At San Matías Street, we find the **church of San Matías** (Saint Matthew). Dating from the XVIth century, it has two interesting plateresque gates by Sebastián Alcántara. In its Gothic inside, we can draw attention to the beautiful XVIIIth century Baroque High Altar, with two sculptures by Risueño (the impressive and masterly Saint John of God) and several paints by Bocanegra. It is called imperial because the Emperor Charles V favoured and furnished it, on the basis of his devotion to Saint Matthew, as he was the saint of his birth day.

Walking down San Matías Street, we get to **Campillo**, a square that Cervantes mentioned in his Quixote, as a place with an unbelievable atmosphere. Walking up the street now, we get to the place where the Great Captain lived and died (1515), opposite to a Franciscane Monastery (currently the premises of the general captaincy) and next to a Discalced Carmelite convent. Here is the start of the beautiful Pavaneras Street, with its mansions. Among them, we remark the **Casa del Padre Juárez** (House of Father Juárez), where the eminent Granadine theologian and philosopher was born in (1548), and that currently houses the **Archive of the Chancellery.**

The **Casa de los Tiros** is next to it (20, Pavaneras Street). An interesting civil

Trips round the city

building of the XVIth century, with a stone façade by way of tower with merlons covered with a roof. There are five mythological statues in the façade, as well as the Coat-of-Arms of the Granadine Venegas family, that inhabited and improved this building. The most remarkable elements of the inside are the quiet courtyard and the impressive *Cuadra Dorada,* a hall with a grandiose ceiling carved with

The Cristo de los favores *(Christ of the mercies) distributes its reputation as a miracle-worker from the* Campo del Príncipe *(Field of the Prince).*

polychrome and golden figures. This place is used by the *Junta de Andalucía* (Andalusian Autonomous Government) for recitals and as a conference hall. In the building there is also a museum of Granadine history

The Casa de los Tiros (House of the shots) is one of the last witness of the magnificent past of the Realejo quarter.

and craftsmanship, with interesting documents and an excellent public newspaper archive where papers from 1764 and on are kept.

The popular **quarter of the Realejo** starts here, and it is very advisable to strolling around its streets and capture its peculiar atmosphere. One can even go up to the very feet of the *Torres Bermejas* (Red Towers) of get to the **Antequeruela,** a place that was probably populated by the refugees came from Antequera. One of the most hidden *carmenes* in that area is the **Manuel de Falla Museum-House.** This beautiful carmen, located in an unparalleled place, guard a large amount of memories of the eminent compositor, native of Cádiz. Manuel de Falla lived and worked here from the early nineteen twenties until 1939, when he emigrated to Argentina. Together with his piano and personal belongings, we can find a side look at the Spain of that time. One stone throw away, there is its archive and library, accommodated in a modern centre of studies.

Walking down the Antequeruela, there is the **church of San Cecilio** (Saint Cecil). Built in the XVIth century, it has a Plateresque gate and a gorgeous Mudejar coffered ceiling. It is dedicated to the Patron Saint of Granada and reportedly occupies the site of the mosque of Antequeruela. Interesting staircase and artistic altarpiece. Also remarkable oils on board and sculptures. Its façade has been recently decorated with paints.

The **Campo del Príncipe** (Field of the Prince) lays at its feet: a beautiful Granadine square where the stone image of the *Cristo de los Favores* (Christ of Mercies) (1640), believed to make miracles, is. The square, flanked by the **Palacio del Almirante de Aragón** (Palace of the Admiral of Aragon), has popular and typical flavour. It is one of the best *tapeo* places in Granada, especially in hot summer nights.

There is an interesting group of convents near the Campo del Príncipe. That of **Santa Catalina** (Saint Catherine) gives way to the steep *Cuesta del Realejo* and guards valuable art works. The convent of the **Comendadoras de Santiago** (Commanders of Santiago) was founded by the queen Isabella the Catholic (1501) in the house of the first archbishop of Granada and has a Baroque altarpiece and some images that are taken around Granada in the Easter processions. It is also a very popular place with the lovers of the sweets made by the nuns. **Los Ángeles** (The Angels) is humble, but guards some important religious images.

Walking down these streets of the Realejo, get to the **Church of Santo Domingo.** It was part of the **Monastery of** *Santa Cruz la Real* (The Royal Holy Cross), founded by the Catholic Monarchs the same year of the conquest of Granada at the **huerta de Almanxarra,** which was the leisure state of queen Aisha, the wife of Muley Hasan (Mulhacen) and mother of Muhammad XII Abu 'Abd Allah. This church is a transition from Gothic style into the Renaissance and has an excellent Baroque tabernacle dating from the end of the XVIIth century. Collection of paintings and a silver sheet Virgin of the Rosary, venerated by the Spanish Navy in its profusely adorned lady chapel, with tributes to the Battle of Lepanto. Part of the convent, with its wide and elegant courtyard, is now used as a hall of residence. The Dominican manage the facilities and the church.

In front of it, there is a good statue of the most eminent Granadine Dominican: Fray Luis de Granada. This quarter was one of the most important of the Arab Granada. There are still traces of that time, like the **Casa de los Girones,** in the front street of the **Church of Santo Domingo,** and the *Cuarto Real* (Royal Hall) **of Santo Domingo.** The hall of a former Arab palace with interesting Nasrid decorations, imitating the Comares tower at the Alhambra. It is currently being restored in order to open it to the public. From this mansion, that was a balcony above the poplar groves of the Darro, go down to the *Carrera de la Virgen.*

The **basilica of the** *Virgen de las Angustias* (Virgin of the Anguish) is located in this promenade, which is one of the busiest in Granada. This Baroque temple of the XVIIth century has a splendid brick façade flanked by two superb towers. Gate of Marble from Elvira and very rich decoration in the inside: there are marbles of different colours, polychrome sculptures, paintings and different details that are included in the peaks of the Granadine Baroque. The High Altarpiece from the

Trips round the city

■ Parque de las Ciencias
Avda. del Mediterráneo, s/n. ℘ 958 131 900
Entry: 2,40 €
⊙ Tuesday to Saturday from 10 to 19 h
Sunday and holidays from 10 to 15 h
From 15 to 30 of september, closed.

■ Huerta de San Vicente - Museo García Lorca
℘ 958 258 466.
Entry: 1,80 €
⊙ Summer (April-September)
Morning from 10 to 13 h
Afternoon from 17 to 20 h
⊙ Winter (Oct-March)
Morning from 10 to 13 h
Afternoon from 16 to 19 h
Monday, closed.
Wednesday not holidays, free.

XVIIIth century is profusely decorated with marble and is opened in the centre, thus showing the Chamber of the Virgen de las Angustias, with a richly jewelled image of the Patron Virgin of Granada, of which Granadines are very devout.
Behind the church, the waters of the river Darro run now under the vaults over which the Acera del Darro goes. At the end of this street, the mouth of the Darro into the Genil can be seen, as well as the Arab bridge above it, now used only by pedestrians. Up the river Genil, you will walk across the *Jardines del Salón* (Gardens of the Hall) and *de la Bomba* (of the Bomb), where years ago the Corpus Christy Fair was celebrated and where some beautiful mansions can be seen. Ángel Ganivet once lived in a mill near there. These gardens where also the starting point of the old tram to the Sierra Nevada, just like the road to the mountains, planned by the Duque of San Pedro Galatino, starts there today.
From the mouths of the Darro, follow the water down the Genil foe a while and get to the **Palacio de Congresos** (Congress Centre): an impressive building in pink granite and green serpentine that has a large congress hall, exhibit premises and the most varied services for meetings and celebrations.
Hidden behind a few trees in the vast flat area outside the congress centre, there is the **Hermitage of San Sebastián** (Saint Sebastian). It is one of the oldest and most peculiar monuments in Granada. It was once a *morabito,* an Arab place for prayer by the river, and was built at the beginning of the XIIIth century. Interesting dome and horseshoe arch in the entrance. The tradition says that, in 1492, the Catholic Monarchs met Muhammad XII Abu 'Abd Allah before its doors. It was later transformed into a Christian chapel and is still used as a temple.
Right in front of its door, the city has erected a statue to its last Nasrid king. And at its back, overwhelmed by blocks of flats, there are the remains of the

Trips round the city

Alcazar Genil. It once was a great palace with gardens that extended from the river to the plain. There is still a tower with decorated rooms of the time of Yusuf I. It was used as outskirts lodging for the princes and belonged to queen Aisha.

After crossing the **Camino de Ronda**, trying not to look, not to suffer the contrast between the beauty seen during the tour and the mediocre town planning of the area, we get to the Park of the Sciences. A recently created scientific museum where touching is allowed. Furthermore, most of the departments of the park (explore, biosphere, eureka, etc.) require visitors to manipulate and get involved. A good planetarium with its own programs.

Before going back to the start point, one may follow Arabial Street until **García Lorca Park** and visiting the *Huerta de San Vicente* (Saint Vincent Garden). **Museum-house of García Lorca.** The poet and his family used to spend summers there. The decoration chose by the family before the war has been maintained, and there are many souvenirs of the poet. Walk back to the city centre across the quarters of Gracia, the Magdalena and Bib Rambla.

ITINERARY V
THE NORTHERN AREA OF THE OUTSKIRTS

For this tour, go the Plaza Nueva, just like in the first and second itineraries. From there, follow **Elvira Street.** This street, named after the old town, goes along the western side of the Albaicin, and is the perfect example of the town planning of the centre before the construction of the Gran Vía.
At the start of the street, there is the *Hospitalicos,* a Baroque church built onto an

> *The Royal Hospital is a conglomerate of architectural stiles that wake up your senses.*

Trips round the city

Entrance gate to the Cartuja.

■ **Monasterio de la Cartuja**
✆ 958 161 932.
Entry: 1,80 €
⏰ Morning from 10 to 13 h. Sunday morning from 10 to 12 h
⏰ Summer (April-Sept.) Afternoon from 16 to 20 h
⏰ Winter (Oct-March) Afternoon from 15:30 to 18 h

Augustinian convent housed by what once was a military hospital. A bit further, the Calderería comes down the upper Albaicin and joins Elvira Street in front of the place where once stood the **Arab palace of Cetti Meriem**. There are many traditional shops and antique dealers in the area.

Then the street goes behind the church of the *Sagrado Corazón* (Sacred Heart), the church of Santiago (Saint James), where the Inquisition once had it headquarters, and then to the **Church of** *San Andrés* (Saint Andrew).

A stone throw away, there is the majestic *Puerta de Elvira* (Gate of Elvira). Dating from the XIth century, it was the main and one of the oldest entrances to the Arab Granada. It opened the way to the ancient Elvira and its sides were united to the walls that went up to the Albaicin and closed the city in the west.

Around the Puerta de Elvira, there are: the former **Convent of the Mercedarian,**

The Cartuja, the greatest exponent of Baroque.

Trips round the city

now transformed in a military building; the **church of Saint Ildephonse,** also dating from the XVIth century and with a *Mudejar* tower and a Renaissance front by Diego de Siloe; and the *Campo del Triunfo.* This is a large flat area now occupied by gardens that used to be bigger. In it, there was a famous Arab cemetery with a Visigoth church, as well as two bullrings and a scaffold where the famous Granadine heroine Mariana Pineda died. The **monument to the Immaculate Conception** is in an outstanding place, in front of a light fountain built in the nineteen seventies. This monument was carved in the XVIIth century by Alonso de Mena, and consists of a profusely worked pillar on top of which stands the crowned Virgin, surrounded by rays of light. The *Hospital Real* (Royal Hospital) is a bit further *(Cuesta del Hospicio)*. This former hospital founded by the Catholic Monarchs in 1504 outside of the walls of the Arab city, was not only for war wounded soldiers, but also for "innocents", poor people and pilgrims. The Renaissance building has hints of the best Elizabethan style, a Baroque front done in marble from Sierra Elvira, Plateresque windows, magnificent courtyards and *Mudejar* coffered ceilings. Today, it is the one of the premises of the **University of Granada,** and therefore can be visited during academic hours. In the first floor, there is the library where bibliographic gems are conserved, together with a vast documental archive of the

Monument to Fray Luis of Granada, a monk who had a great influence in the city.

university. Going up the Real de Cartuja Street, we get to another traditional quarter of Granada. Not far from there one can visit the **Capucine Convent,** very popular with local devout to Fray Leopoldo de Alpandeire; the Faculty of Medicine; the new Bullring and the **Cartuja University Campus.**

The name of this campus comes from the plots where it is located, which belong to the **Cartuja.** The works of this impressive monument started at the beginning of the XVIth century in plots that belonged to the Great Captain. The slow progress of the works enabled the mixture of styles: the sober Renaissance Monastery, with its courtyard, refectory, capitulary hall and quarters contrasts with the Baroque church. The inside is the peak of the "white" Andalusian Baroque.

The hills of Ainadamar, today occupied by several faculties,

The García Lorca Park is one of the most romantic and evocative sites in Granada.

are behind the Cartuja. There used to be a famous irrigation ditch that supplied the city with water from Alfacar.
By the end of the XIXth century, a neo-Arab style Jesuit novitiate and *colegio máximo* was built. The **Observatory of the Cartuja** is also there. Under its peculiar astronomic dome, instruments used in the past are kept, by way of museum. The observatory is specialized in the seismological monitoring of the area.

Historical itineraries are those designed to visit the monuments according to the time of its construction and, obviously, their style. One would include the Arab Granada (Alminar de San José, walls, Bañuelo, Alhambra, Corral del Carbón, etc.), another would be for the Christian Renaissance Granada (Santa Isabel la Real, Royal Hospital, Royal Chapel, Saint Jerome, the Cathedral), another for *Mudejar* towers (Saint Bartholomew, the Savior, Saint Andrew, Saint Ildephonse, etc.), then the Baroque Granada (San John of God, Saint Dominic), the Romantic Granada, the modern Granada…

Every spring, nature bursts in every corner of Granada.

Trips round the city

Itineraries with a name of their own. Another way to visit a city is through the eyes of the eminent men and women who once inhabited it. To do so, itineraries may be created to visit the places linked to people who were born or lived in Granada, and who excelled in holiness, literature, war, politics, etc.

The co-patron saint of Granada, Saint John of God, arrived from Portugal and used to sell books in Elvira Street. He wandered around *Casa de Agreda* (lower Albaicin), created his hospital in Lucena Street and died in the house of the Pisa's, his body being buried at the magnificent **basilica of Saint John of God.** Next to it, a monumental hospital and a modern health facility keep the labour of the saint alive. Similar ascetic itineraries may be created around the figures of Saint John of the Cross, Saint John of Avila, Fray Leopoldo de Alpandeire, Fray Luis de Granada, Andrés Manjón, etc. The Granadine writers are not less numerous: from the "Gongorian" poet Soto de Rojas *(Carmen* at Pagés Street, Albaicin) to the contemporary winner of the Cervantes Prize, Francisco Ayala. Obviously, Federico García Lorca shines with its own light among them.

The Lorca route in Granada includes the high school where he studied, the gathering of "El rinconcillo", the Art

■ **Cartuja observatory**
Cartuja Campus (next to the Faculty of Arts).
University
✆ 958 201 033

■ **Parque García Lorca**
C/ Arabial, 41.
⏱ From 8 to 23 h.

■ **Mill where Ángel Ganivet used to live**
Cuesta de los Molinos, s/n. ✆ 958 220 157

The heart of Granada is open to let one thousand water channels cross it to feed clear water fountains and dreaming gardens.

Trips round the city

Centre, San Miguel del Albaicin, and dozens of places shown here and there in his poems and theatre plays. Almost all the ways end at the **García Lorca Park** sited around the *Huerta de San Vicente,* the summer residence of the García Lorca family in the outskirts of Granada. Many evocative literary and historical souvenirs of the poet are exhibited there. The itinerary in memory of Ángel Ganivet includes the **mill** where he once lived, which keeps part of the old industrial structure. Currently a centre of ethnological investigations with a dynamic exhibit room has been installed there. The beautiful sculpture of the writer at the Alhambra forest is also worth seeing. Its grave is in the Granadine cemetery and any corner of the old city livens up memories of his book *Granada la bella* (Granada the Beautiful).

The Alhambra starts the journey across this magic city.

The musicians related to Granada make a particular arpeggio of itineraries. From the memories of Debussy, Glinka, Albéniz, Agustín Lara and many other whose music was inspired by Granada, to the local masters, like Francisco Alonso or Ángel Barrios, who has its own museum at the *Polinario* of the Alhambra. There is also an outstanding figure here: Manuel de Falla.

The **Museum House of Manuel de Falla** guards not only an intimate collection of personal belongings of the musician born in Cadiz, but also all the charm and the hidden mysticism of his creative and vital atmosphere. The once Empress of France, Eugenia de Montijo, is remembered in a humble grey memorial tablet in its natal home, in Gracia Street. Alonso Cano and the rest of the *imagineros* (artists who carved religious statues) of the famous Granadine school composite and itinerary that includes: the tower of the Cathedral, where Cano used to live while he was working in the temple; his home in Santa Paula Street, his sculpture at the Sagrario gate, his excellent paints and sculptures at the Cathedral, the Museum of Fine Arts, the Immaculate Conception in the Sacristy of the Cathedral, and a long trail of images distributed among the temples, many of them are used in the Easter processions.

There is a beautiful statue of Mariana Pineda, the heroine of

Panoramic view of the Alhambra with the background of the Sierra Nevada.

freedom, at the square named after her, and a commemorative tile marks the place where she was executed, near the Arch of Elvira. Other itineraries can be created on the basis of the life of other renowned Granadine people, like Álvaro de Bazán, the champion of the Batlle of Lepanto; Martínez de la Rosa, Prime Minister and famous writer; Francisco Suárez, the prestigious jurist; the painters Rodríguez Acosta and Manuel Gómez Moreno, etc.

NATURAL, SCIENTIFIC AND DOCUMENTAL ITINERARIES

Crying hidden water, said the poet about Granada. The water itinerary in Granada is a beautiful labyrinth of hidden streams appearing here and there in many fountains, and showing its urban endeavour in the many cisterns scattered in the old Granada. Worth-visiting cisterns de Trillo, de Rodrigo del Campo, del Rey, de las tomasas, de la Plaza de San Nicolás… Not to miss fountains: the Leones at the Alhambra, the Batallas, of Plaza Nueva, of the *paseo de los Tristes,* of the *gigantones* at Bib Rambla… Also visit the *pilares,* del Toro, at Plaza Nueva; of Elvira street, next to the Arch of Elvira; of the Cathedral, opposite San Jerónimo street… Also, water runs down the small ditches of the Alhambra, the Partal and the Generalife, goes still in ponds and cisterns, livens gardens up, nurtures massive trees and slowly goes down to the river plain. The bell of the Vela de la Alhambra still rings every evening, like it used to do in old times, to regulate the water flow in the irrigation channels of the river plain. Scientific and documental itineraries pass by the Sciences' Park, the Observatory of the Cartuja, the museums of the faculties of Sciences and Pharmacy, the Archive of the Royal Chancellery, the City Archive, etc.

Where to eat

The gastronomy in Granada is as diverse as its history. From *casas de comidas* (affordable home-style restaurants) or taverns to international take away restaurants, so popular among youngsters; from university refectories to luxury restaurants, the possibilities in Granada are numerous. Seating at one table is not enough to get to know the multiple aspects of the Granadine gastronomy. It is necessary to visit its restaurants and taverns, to go for *tapas* in its inns and bars, to have breakfast in its coffee houses, drink a caña (barrel beer in a glass) in its *fisgones* or cellars and stay up a bit late in its late hours clubs. There are delightful dishes, *tapas* and drinks everywhere. Also, if you wish to take a deep approach to Granadine flavours, do not forget to take a look at the market, queue in a *churros* stall, eat some prickly pears in a street stall or search shops for products from the Alpujarra or other Granadine shires.

Granada shares many dishes with other areas of Andalusia: *gazpacho,* well crushed and not so thick as *salmorejo,* the *ajo blanco* with almond flour, the *papas a lo pobre* (poor style potatoes), *Nasrid* lamb, etc.

Where to eat

However, the most genuine Granadine gastronomy is, of course, based on the excellent natural products of the province. The smoked ham of Trévelez; the prawns and fish from Motril, delicious in *moraga;* wild asparagus of Huétor Tájar, excellent with scrambled eggs; avocados from Almuñécar... The gastronomic affinity among them is remarkable: the famous *habas con jamón* (broad beans with ham) mix the product from the Alpujarra and the vegetable from the river plain; the *migas granadinas* go well with all kinds of chunks; and the coastal avocados make an excellent potato salad with boiled potatoes and prawns from Motril. An of course, there are the exceptional specialities, like the Sacromonte omelette, with different kinds of *chacinas* (cured pork meat products), the pumpkin *salamandroña,* the *remojón granadino* with cod, oranges and black olives; etc.

Other Granadine products that enjoy a deserved fame are: *morcilla* (blood sausage) and *chorizo* from Los Montes, very suitable for *cocidos* and barbecues; *lomo de horza* (dry cured pork loin) from the Baza shire; peaches from Purullena; pears from the river plain; chestnuts from Guéjar Sierra; figs and *pan de higo* (dried fig tart) from Contraviesa; fresh cheese from Alhama; persimmons from the valley of Lecrín; the custard apples from the coast, etc.

Gazpacho *(cold tomato based soup) is one of the most traditional dishes of Andalusian cooking*.

SACROMONTE SPINACHES

Ingredients. 4 servings:

*1.5 kg of fresh spinaches
Water, salt
200 gr of non-toasted almond
4 tbsp of oil
A few saffron threads
50 gr. of raisins
1 tsp of vinegar
Ground white pepper
4 slices of fried bread
2 garlic cloves
2 tbsp of bread crumbs*

- Carefully wash the spinaches and rinse them with cool water, then boil them in plenty salty water.
- After boiling and draining the leaves, chop them with a knife.
- Blanch the almonds in boiling water and then fry them in two spoons of oil with two chopped garlic cloves and the bread crums.
- Once fried, mix it with the saffron and crush it in the mortar.
- Sauté the spinaches in the remaining oil and add the mix in the mortar and the chopped raisins. Add vinegar and a bit of pepper (maybe a pinch of salt).
- Serve it with the fried bread.

COCKTAILS, CAÑAS, AND OTHER DRINKS

The beer from Granada is named after its most emblematic monument. The company has gone one step further and the regular lager is now accompanied by the "negra" (stout) and the recently created "Alhambra, reserva 1925", elaborated with special care.

The province of Granada provides its capital with several kinds of wine. The closest one is that of Huétor Vega. This young wine is almost impossible to find, so visitors will have to go to the village, some 5 km far from Granada, to savour its real aroma. Bottled wines, which have eventually become acceptable reds for meats, also arrive from the area of Campocámara and Baza. However, the most famous wine in Granada is the *costa*, a fruity wine with a brown-deep red colour, a fine palate and very appropriate for the smoked ham from the Alpujarra. Despite its name (*costa* is coast in Spanish) it is not only produced by the Mediterranean, but also even in some inland rags, at the Contraviesa. It is well known that the wine must not leave those rags, as it loses most of its flavour. However, in some establishments, like La Mancha and Bodegas Castañeda, in Joaquín Costa street, the wine is served in good condition. It is even bottled, Barranco Oscuro being the most remarkable.

Where to eat

Among the spirits manufactured in Granada we must mention the *ron pálido de la costa* (pale rum from the coast), a wonder made out of sugar cane. There is also the **craft *pacharán*** (sloe berry liquor) made in Monachil, in the skirt of Sierra Nevada and a non-alcoholic **liqueur of custard apples** that will soon achieve its best performance.

FOR MUGS AND CUPS

Breakfast and afternoon snack in Granada is one of those small pleasures suitable for any pocket and that leave a nice recall. *Churros* are great for any of them. In Granada they are wheel-like, known as *tejeringos* in other places and as *tallos* in Jaen. The *churros* are cut from the big wheel and are wider than closed ring ones, but narrower that *porras* from Madrid and have no grooves. There are several good places for *churros:* Café Fútbol at 6, Mariana Pineda square; Churrería Alhambra and Bib-Rambla at Bib-Rambla square, etc. But in the mornings, you can also get freshly fried and affordable *churros* in street stalls (by the market doors, Romanilla, Caleta, etc.) and take them to the closest coffee houses, where this practice is normal. Among the traditional Granadine sweets the most popular are the ***piononos*** from Santa Fe, a roll of sponge cake soaked in liqueur with a coin of cream on top, and the *soplillos de la Alpujarra*, some kind of petrified egg mousse with almonds in the inside. And do not forget the ***pestiños*** from **Vélez Benaudalla,** the ***roscos*** from Loja, the *tarta real* from Motril, the *cuajado de carnaval* and a long list of diverse sweets, most of them with a remote *Morisco* origin.

The virgin olive oil is very appreciated for toasts of *mollete*, a type of very soft white bread. However, the most famous Granadine breads are those of Alfacar and Caniles.

There are also convent sweets, especially in Christmas: the ***huevo mol*** of Franciscan nuns of San Antón, the ***mantecados*** (cakes similar to shortbread) of the nuns of Zafra, the ***glaseados*** of Santiago, etc shall not be missed.

Terraces outside liven up at dusk.

Where to eat

Granada enjoys a wide and diverse variety of gastronomic styles.

OUR SELECTION OF RESTAURANTS

There is a wide range of recommendable restaurants in Granada. From the *casas de comidas* (cheap restaurants) with menus under 6 €, to the creative and sophisticated restaurants, the city opens its kitchens to the visitors for them to choose according to their situation and, that is for sure, can enjoy the southern cookery. The following is a list of suggestions intended only as an advice. The restaurants are grouped by areas.
Most of the establishments mentioned below have a bar area where you can have a drink or a snack while you wait to be seated, or just go for a *tapa*.

City centre

El Claustro
Gran Vía de Colón, 31.
✆ *958 805 740.*
✗ *Never.* ♠ ♠
Signature cooking with special attention to Granadine products.

Cunini
Plaza de la Pescadería, 14.
✆ *958 250 777 / 958 267 587.*
☺ *From 12 to 16 and from 20 to 24 h. Reservations recommended.*
✗ *Never.* ♠ ♠
A classic in Granada for quality fish and seafood. Excellent fried dishes, special potato salad and a particular touch in some recipes. A very good place for fish *tapas*.

Chikito
Campillo Square, 9.
✆ *958 223 364.*
☺ *From 13 to 16 and from 20 to 23.30 h.* ✗ *Wednesday.* ♠ ♠
Traditional Andalusian cookery and also good for *tapas*. Located in the former Café Alameda, the site of the famous gathering "El Rinconcillo", where Manuel de Falla, García Lorca, Fernández

Where to eat

Almagro and other writers met. There is a commemorative tile in the façade. The dinning room is not very spacious, but the bull tail and the beef *churrasco* is worth trying.

SEVILLA
Oficios, 3 (opposite to the Royal Chapel). ℘ 958 221 223.
⏰ *From 13 to 16 and from 20 to 23.30 h. Late al fresco terrace from 24 to 3 h (with drinks and sweets and live classic music).*
✖ *Monday and Sunday night.* ♠ ♠
Regional and modern dishes. Traditional Granadine cook. Wood stove. Traditional dishes: *Sopa sevillana* (Seville soup), *Cordero al pastoril* (shepherd's lamb).

EL DIVÁN DEL TAMARIT
Puerta Real, 1. Olmedo building, La Manigua y C/ Escudo del Carmen, 6 ℘ 958 226 293 / 958 223 000.
⏰ *From 13 to 16 and from 20 to 24 h.*
✖ *Never.* ♠ ♠
Business atmosphere, with professionals, journalists and businesspersons. Basque cookery with southern hints.

TAVARES
Carrera de la Virgen, 6. ℘ 958 226 769.
International establishment, well located and decorated with great care.

LAS TRÉBEDES
(Restaurant of El Corte Inglés). Carrera del Genil, 20-22. ℘ 958 223 240.
⏰ *From 13 to 16:30 h.*
✖ *Nights and bank holidays.* ♠ ♠
Southern cookery with excellent raw materials.

CASA SALVADOR
Duende, 6. ℘ 958 255 009.
✖ *Sunday night, Mondays and July.*
Regional cookery Affordable menus.

MESÓN GREGORIO
Paseo de los Basilios, 3. ℘ 958 815 007.
Good traditional dishes from Madrid (snails, *callos*, potato salas...) and affordable prices. Al fresco terrace.

Modern area of the Camino de Ronda

LA ESTANCIA
Párraga, 9. ℘ 958 251 836.
⏰ *From 13:30 to 16:30 and from 20 to 24 h.* ✖ *Never.* ♠ ♠
Mediterranean fish-based dishes.

LAS TINAJAS
Martínez Campos, 17. ℘ 958 254 393.
⏰ *From 11:30 to 16:30 and from 20 to 24 h.* ♠ ♠
One of the specialists in Granadine cookery, despite it is not as affordable as it used to be. Its Granadine tasting menu is a must for those willing to know the traditional dishes of the region: *gazpacho*, *habas con jamón* (broad beans with ham), *rape mozárabe* (Mozarab monkfish) and *tarta morisca* (Morisco cake). Its famous hake loins filled with salmon au gratin are also part of the Andalusian cookery. Open everyday.

MARIQUILLA
Lope de Vega, 2. ℘ 958 521 632.
✖ *Monday and Sunday night.* ♠ ♠
Signature cook with southern notes. Best dishes: *ajo blanco* with grapes and lamb stew.

CALADERO DEL BACALAO
Pedro Antonio de Alarcón, 34. ℘ 958 265 061. ♠ ♠
Cod-based cookery, as well as signature dishes with international touches. Careful service.

Where to eat

MESÓN ANTONIO PÉREZ
Pintor Rodríguez Acosta, 1.
✆ 958 288 079

KUDAMM
Pedro Antonio de Alarcón, 36.
✆ 958 251 718.
Obispo Hurtado, 18.
✆ 958 253 264.
Pedro Antonio de Alarcón, 3.
✆ 958 252 151.
⌚ *From 13:30 to 16:30 and from 21 to 00:30 h. On Saturdays and Sundays the closing hour is 1 am.*
✖ *Never.* ♠

Three different cooking styles in inviting backgrounds: Andalusian, German and Italian.

POETAS ANDALUCES
Pedro Antonio de Alarcón, 13.
✆ 958 263 050.

A traditional establishment that keeps part of its past charm.

PEPE TORO
Camino de Ronda, 101.
✆ 958 279 865.
⌚ *From 13:30 to 16:30 and from 20 to 24 h.*
✖ *Sunday night.* ♠

Influences of the Alpujarra and Andalusia.

PICCOLA ITALIA
Obispo Hurtado, 13.
✆ 958 259 678.
⌚ *From 13 to 16 and from 20:30 to 23.30 h.* ✖ *Sunday.* ♠ ♠

Elaborated dishes inspired in Italian food.

LOS SANTANDERINOS
Albahaca, 3. (Urbanización Jardín de la Reina). ✆ 958 128 335.

One of the establishments favouring contrast: Andalusian cookery shares its space with high quality traditional northern meats and dishes. Especially remarkable are the potajes montañeses and the Cantabrian fish.

From the Realejo to the Alhambra

HORNO DE SANTIAGO
Plaza de los Campos, 8.
✆ 958 223 476.
⌚ *From 13:30 to 16 and from 20 to 24 h.* ✖ *Sunday night.* ♠ ♠

Mundane culinary creations and business lunches. Crab and cod based creations.

MESÓN ANTONIO
Ecce Homo, 6 (next to Campo del Príncipe). ✆ 958 229 599.
✖ *Sundays, July and August.*

Northern home-style cook. Very nice atmosphere.

PIZZERÍA LA NINFA
Campo del Príncipe, 14.
✆ 958 229 630. ✖ *Tuesday.*

Easy-going establishment, located in an ancient building with several storeys. Speciality in Italian pasta, sauces and other dishes served in Granadine pottery. It is also a hostel.

COLOMBIA
Antequeruela Baja, 1.
✆ 958 227 433/ 958 227 434.
✖ *Sundays.*

Traditional Andalusian cookery with a beautiful panoramic view of Granada. Also international and regional cook. Speciality in *sopa de D. Juan* (don Juan soup), bull tail and house dishes.

CARMEN DE SAN MIGUEL
Pl. Torres Bermejas, 3. ✆ 958 226 723.
✖ *Sundays in summer.*

National and regional cookery in a balcony above the Realejo. Traditional dish: Lobster salad with oysters.

LA MIMBRE
Bosque de Alhambra (Generalife entrance). ✆ 958 222 276.
⌚ *From 10 to 16:30 and from 20:30 to 00:30 h.* ✖ *Never.* ♠ ♠

Where to eat

Granadine gastronomy, famous for its Sacramento omelette. The perfect place for an out of doors dinner in a charming spot.

PARADOR NACIONAL DE TURISMO SAN FRANCISCO
Real de la Alhambra, s/n.
℘ 958 221 440.
⌚ From 13 to 16 and from 20:30 to 23 h. ✗ Never. ♠ ♠
Lovely terrace in front of the Generalife. Occasionally, live classic guitar music. International and Andalusian cookery.

Albaicín and Sacromonte

SAMARKANDA
Calderería Vieja, 3.
℘ 958 210 004.
⌚ From 13 to 16:30 and from 19 to 00.30 h. ✗ Never. ♠ ♠
Lebanese-origin Arab cookery. Quality for exotic palates.

EL LEÓN
Pan, 2.
Affordable meals. For fast and affordable meals. Traditional plain but quality dish of the day.

Nights are especially suitable for enjoying dinning under the stars.

TORRES BERMEJAS
Plaza Nueva, 6. ℘ 958 223 116.
✗ Never.
International cookery. Speciality in Sacromonte omelette and broad beans with ham. Good terrace.

MIRADOR DE MORAYMA
Pianista García Carrillo, 2.
℘ 958 228 290.
Enjoy a good dinner and admire the Alhambra. A must go for romantics.

LAS TOMASAS
Carril de San Agustín (Albaicín).
℘ 958 224 108.
⌚ From 21:30 to 1 h (from middle July to the end of September). Late terrace: from 1 to 2:30 h (for drinks).
✗ Sunday. Better walking than driving. ♠ ♠
A real *carmen* with real sloped terraces for dinning and having a drink outdoors while admiring the Alhambra.

Where to eat

Northern area

Pizzería Altamura
Avda. Andaluces, 2.
✆ 958 272 908.
⏲ From 13:30 to 16:30 h and from 20:30 to 24 h.
✘ Monday and Tuesday. ♠ ♠
Maybe the best in Granada for its quality, price and service. Quality meats and pasta with the genuine Italian touch. Italian food and fine meats.

Rincón de Miguel
Avda. de Andaluces, 2.
✆ 958 292 978.
⏲ From 13 to 17 and from 20:30 to 23.30 h. *✘ Sunday.* ♠ ♠
Modern establishment with contemporary dishes.

Exotic cooking has also its space among the possibilities that Granada, as a multicultural city, has to offer.

El Cenador
Doctor Olóriz, 13.
✆ 958 277 039 / 958 209 724.
✘ Sundays and bank holidays.
Home-style cook, quiet atmosphere.

La Ermita de la Plaza de Toros
Avda. Doctor Olóriz, 25 (Bullring premises).
✆ 958 290 257 / 958 276 308.
Modern place, careful cook and *tapas*, taurine decoration and lots of charm for bullfighting lovers.

Velázquez
Emilio Orozco, 1.
✆ 958 280 109.
✘ Sunday. ♠ ♠
Diverse cookery with southern hints.

In the outskirts

Ruta del Veleta
Road to the Sierra Nevada, km 5.4 (Cenes de la Vega).
✆ 958 486 134 / 958 486 381.
⏲ From 13 to 16:30 h and from 20 to 24 h.
✘ Sunday night. ♠ ♠
Probably the peak of Granadine gastronomy. Quite original Andalusian dishes and international cookery. Specialities: *salmorejo*, Granadine garlic soup, partridge with onions, etc.

Los Pinillos
Ctra. de la Sierra, km 6.
✆ 958 486 109.

Pizzería La Chimenea
Camino Atajadero, s/n. Huétor Vega (5 km from Granada).
✆ 958 300 843.
Delicious *roscas* and cheese with avocado in a very peculiar atmosphere, rescued from a former tobacco drying hut.

Where to eat

The merry and sunny days in Granada invite to have a cookout.

Outdoors dinning

Beautiful views and quality food.

JARDINES ALBERTO
Alhambra / Generalife.
958 224 818.
From 13 to 16 and from 20 to 24 h.
Sunday night. ♠ ♠
Mediterranean dishes with a modern touch in a typical Granadine garden.

MIRADOR DE AIXA
Carril de San Agustín, 2 (Albaicín).
958 228 030.
From 21 h to 2 am.
Winter.

An ancient *carmen* open to the public at night. For *tapas,* dinner or drinks, right opposite to the Alhambra. Very good *sangria.* Better walking than driving.

EL AGUA
Placeta Aljibe de Trillo, 7. (Albaicín).
958 224 356.
A narrow *carmen* in the Albaicin transformed into a wine house. Wines, cold meats and a good fondue at the balconies opening into the Alhambra.

As well as the above mentioned restaurants, there is a long list of Chinese restaurants, hamburger bars, take away and fast food establishments, sandwich bars etc.

Tapas and drinks

A city, a region or a nation cannot be well known until one has drunk its wine and tasted its food. Granada is famous for its generous *tapeo* (eating *tapas),* offered at no charge with the drinks. And there are several areas to enjoy this lifestyle inside the urban background. Its wide variety, comprising *conchas, raciones* (portions), *medias raciones* (half portions), *pinchos* (small tapas), etc., enables the tasting of a mixture of masterly seasoned Mediterranean food.
Tapas are the perfect company for the cañas or the drinks, as well as a brief palatable display window of the establishment. Many bars are known for their *tapas* and their flavour and originality tell more about the establishment than any other possible advertising. In some of them, you may order any of those offered in the menu. Just ask for it. Almost all the bars that do not serve breakfast open their kitchens for tapeo in the early afternoon until 4 pm, and then from 8 pm until midnight. In café-bars, kitchens may be open fron 7 am. The average price of a beer with *tapa* is: 150/175 pts.
The establishments mentioned are those that have only a bar for *tapeo* and, maybe, a few tables or barrels

for resting the *tapa,* but are not classified as restaurants. Therefore, for a complete list of *tapeo* establishments, you should add the bar of those who were mentioned as restaurants above.

AREAS AND ESTABLISMENTS

City centre, Navas street, Moras Street and Puerta Real (all the buses)

At the very administrative and business centre of the city, there are many bars where the famous Granadine *tapas* can be enjoyed.

Los Diamantes
C/ Navas, 7.
Speciality in fish and seafood. Do not miss fried food, *pil-pil* prawns and eggplants. Beer served in very thin glasses.

Los Manueles
C/ Zaragoza, 2 and 4.
It is in a narrow pedestrian street near the Puerta Real. Sacromonte omelette and broad beans with ham. The food is almost as diverse as the decoration in black iron of the street.

Enrique
Acera de Darro, 8.
At the very Puerta Real, opposite Isabel La Católica Theatre. Ancient traditional inn with an excellent variety of wines. No free *tapas,* but they offer good portions of *chacinas* (cured pork meat products). Closed on Sundays.

San Remo
Puente Castañeda, s/n (a stone throw away from Puerta Real).
Good *tapas* and a certain resemblance to the Paris quartier latin.

Plaza Nueva, Elvira, Carrera del Darro and Paseo de los Tristes (Albaicín minibus)

At the foot of the Alhambra, among its narrow streets and its typical squares, you will find traditional taverns and *fisgones*. Among the many and good ones, we choose:

Bodegas Castañeda
C/ Elvira y Almireceros, 1.
A great variety of wines and the atmosphere of a tavern of the XIXth century.

El León
Pan Street, 1 (next to Elvira street).
The kitchen of this traditional bar is always active. Cheap, fast and good.

Sibari
Plaza Nueva, 3.
Its terrace, like any of the Plaza Nueva, is a must in summer nights. For cold winter days they offer a cup of broth as a liquid *tapa.*

Casa Julio
Hermosa street, 3.
A typical tavern in an improbable street. Delicious fried eggplant.

La Trastienda
Plaza de Cuchilleros, 11.
A former grocer's transformed into the back room of *tapeo.* Very nice in cold nights. Good varied portions of cold stuffed meats and international cheeses.

El Granero de Abrantes
Plaza poeta Luis Rosales, s/n.
It has the charm of the old buildings transformed into inns.

Tapas and drinks

Albaicín (Albaicín minibus)

A walk around the hidden little squares of the intimist streets will amaze you for the welcoming disposition of its people, and, of course, for the rich *tapas* of its bars and cellars that follow each other like the beads of a gastronomic rosary.

LARA
Plaza de San Miguel Bajo.
Good fried food and tasty salads. Its terrace is very busy in summer nights and in winter Sunday mornings.

PAÑERO
Plaza del Aliatar, s/n.
A classic in the Albaicín. Speciality in snails.

TORCUATO
C/ Pagés, 1.
As well as fish, the *tapa* is usually a spoonful of the home-style food prepared for the restaurant.

JUANILLO
Camino del Sacromonte, 81.
Tapas are just as good as the panoramic view from its French windows. Try the *migas*.

Realejo and way down to the river

The Herat of the Realejo is the Campo del Príncipe, one of the most charming Granadines squares, and an invitation to quiet chats and al fresco evenings with locals and strangers by the bars of the taverns or sitting at the terraces. The perfect place for al fresco meals, even in winter. If you order *perdices* (partridges) here, you will get lettuce hearts seasoned with oil and fried garlic.

LOS MARTINETES
The veteran of all the bars in that side of the street. Its croquettes and potato salad are a must.

Tapeo *(eating* tapas) *in Granada is a real pleasure, as well as a deep-rooted habit.*

Tapas and drinks

EL SOTA
Plaza Realejo, 2.
It is named after one of the most famous innkeepers in Granada. Old style *tapas* in a recently reformed establishment. Literary gatherings.

DIÁVOLO
Cementerio Sta. Escolástica, 2.
The novelty in *tapas* among all the traditional bars.

CASA HITA
Paseo del Violón, 9.
Good *tapas,* high quality smoked ham and a wide variety of wines.

University area

The southern end of Pedro Antonio de Alarcón Street, Emperatriz Eugenia, and surrounding areas until the Camino de Ronda make up the young heart of the city. The most diverse bars, pubs, and clubs can be found there. It's the perfect place to start the evening and for night drinks. Among the many establishments our choices are:

Tapeo is the core of the street atmosphere.

JABUGO
Trajano Street (with Sócrates).
Traditional Andalusian bar for eating Ham from Huelva, *morcilla de entraña* (blood sausage) and potato and prawn salad.

DE COSTA A COSTA
Ancha de Gracia, 3.
New, bright and perfect for a good beer with fried fish and fresh seafood.

CINCO NACIONES
Velázquez, 12.
More than 70 national and foreign beers.

PIPOS
Santa Clotilde, 9.
A popular establishment. Speciality in fish and *paella*.

The premises of the bullring benefit from a tempting and lively atmosphere at the tapeo *time.*

Other tapeo areas

Of course, there are many other *tapeo* areas in the city, specially the typical establishments in populous quarters like Zaidín, Chana, Plaza de Toros, Alhamar, etc. where tourists rarely show. If you have a taste for a less snooty atmosphere and time to spend, we recommend you to leave the sightseeing area and sneak in these quarters, where you can judge the quality of the establishment by the number of locals inside it at the aperitif hour.

TENDIDO 1
In the bullring premises.
For *tapas* of Iberian *embutidos* and the house specialities in a typically taurine atmosphere.

EL GRAN TAPEO
Avda. de América, 44 (Zaidín).
The selection of the *tapas* and its presentation has been carefully done. Cookery of the river plain.

LA CUEVA
Road to Madrid, Macarena exit. (3 km. from Granada).
Quality chacinas, Granadine ham and home-made *embutidos*.

Inside Tendido *(Section) 1 of the bullring.*

Tapas and drinks

Bar and bazaar in the Arab quarter of Granada.

Tapas and drinks

Atmosphere in the terraces of the Plaza Nueva *(New Square).*

Shopping in Granada

Granada has a very dynamic and diverse commercial atmosphere. As well as the standard food, decoration and clothing products, the city has a wide range of its own handicrafts (pottery, copper, inlay, etc.) Antiques, flowers, lithographs, etc complete this economic sector, which is one of the most important in the city. In the quarters with a Morisco origin, good imitators of the Arab handicrafts have established their souks, where all kind of items brought from the East are mixed with perfumes and jewels.
Department stores regularly hold Granadine theme seasons, especially in the food and handicrafts sections. While prices are fixed at the department stores, bargaining in the small shops of the city centre is not only allowed, but even advisable, and shopkeepers usually offer discounts to customers.
The opening hours match the tourist hours. Many shops close at midday, but those dedicated to craftsmanship open on Saturdays and Sundays.
The shopping area for tourists goes from the Bibrambla Square to the Plaza Nueva and the Cuesta de Gomérez. The heart of this area is in the site of the former Arab souk and the Medieval silk market: the

Alcaicería. It is in this quarter where the most prestigious shops are, and it is not strange to see modern clothing shops next to traditional ancient deep-rooted establishments at Zacatín pedestrian street and surrounding streets. Nevertheless, moving off the area to the Elvira Street or to the Faculty of Science is advisable, in order to find that "bargain" that lies abandoned in a small and rickety shop, or that item with the same quality, but a lower price.

AREAS AND TYPES OF SHOPS

Department stores and hypermarkets

ALCAMPO
Road to Madrid.
✆ 958 290 316

CARREFOUR
Road to Armilla.
✆ 958 246 413

**HIPERCOR
(EL CORTE INGLÉS)**
C/ Arabial, 97.
✆ 958 208 412

CORTE INGLÉS
Carrera de la Virgen, s/n.
This department store has a permanent section in the ground flour dedicated to Granadine handicrafts and other typical products.

There are also several commercial centres. One of the busiest is the Neptuno Shopping Centre.
The small shops are located in the city centre.

Craftsmanship

Granadine craftsmanship is famous all around Spain. Many are the types of items that have proclaimed this fame, and one is the place where them all merge, creating a colourful craftsmanship souk, just like those of the Moorish times. It is the Medieval Market of the Alcaicería, between the Cathedral and Zacatin Street. Visiting this place is a must, not only for the quantity and quality of the articles sold there, but also for its atmosphere and its appearance inherited from the times when there was the Arab silk market. Other places to go:

FORTUNY
Plaza Fortuny, s/n (Realejo).
Speciality in tissues from the Alpujarras and wool rugs. They have their own designs.

MIMA
Reyes Católicos, 18.
Buy Spanish *mantillas, mantones de Manila* (traditional embroidered silk shawls) and embroidery at the city centre.

MORALES
*Ctra. Gomérez and Bellido, 9.
Plaza Realejo, 15.*
Two famous Granadine guitar makers that make castanets and other instruments, as well as *flamenco* guitars.

FAJALAUZA (MORALES)
Ctra. de Murcia (Albaicín) and San Isidro. Plaza de San Isidro, 5.
The longer established pottery kiln in Granada, which still elaborate the traditional Granadine pottery with a slightly pink background and pictures of birds, flowers and pomegranates in cobalt blue or pale green.

Shopping in Granada

TALLERES DE CUESTA GOMÉREZ
Speciality in Granadine inlay. A real gem.

ESTÉVEZ
Alhóndiga, 39.
The award-winning Granadine lantern maker. Artistic Granadine lanterns in tin and glass.

Jewellery

The most traditional jewel in Granada is a pomegranate worked on a precious metal with garnet grains. They can be found in any size and quality –from costume jewellery to gold– despite the typical version is in silver. A wide and exclusive selection can be found in:

SAN ELOY
Reyes Católicos, 7.

Artisan in his marquetry workshop.

JUAN MANUEL
Ganivet, 8.

ROMERA
Reyes Católicos, 25.
Traditional silversmith in shop windows from the early XXth century.

LUIS BERKEM
Montererría, s/n.
Right the opposite to the previous shop: modern and daring design jewels.

RAFAEL MORENO
Reyes Católicos, 32.
One of the best goldsmiths in Spain. Silver Nasrid-style pieces.

Gastronomy

ANTIGUA CASA HITA
Carrera de la Virgen, 7 and 9.

CASA VÍLCHEZ
Carrera de la Virgen, 17.
Curing and sale of Granadine hams.

MERCADO DE ABASTOS
Plaza San Agustín, s/n.
Vegetables from the river plain and fish from Motril.

AGUAYO
Poeta M. de Góngora.

MUÑOZ RIVAS
Párraga, 7.
℘ *958 262 798.*
Important Granadine wine stores (Contraviesa, Baza, etc.), as well as a wide variety of wines from the entire Andalusia.

FLOR Y NATA
Mesones, 34.
Pastries and chocolate elaborated in their premises, variety of cakes.

LÓPEZ MEZQUITA
Reyes Católicos, 39 and 41.
Delicatessen.

Shopping in Granada

Souvenirs in the raise to the Alhambra.

Casa Isla
Constitución, 18 and Carrera de la Virgen.
Traditional *piononos*.

Convent confectionery

The famous confectionery of Granadine convents may be bought all year round, despite it is in Christmas when people queue to buy these creations that taste heavenly.

Monjas de Santiago
Santiago, 20.

De la Magdalena
Gracia, 7.

De Zafra
Carrera de Darro, 43.

Bernardas
Carrera de Darro, 47.

San Antón
San Antón, 1.

Jerónimas
San Jerónimo, s/n.

Records and books

Urbano
Tablas, 6. ✆ *958 221 103 / 958 252 909.*
Diverse and large stock. Department of bibliographic information.

Librería Científica Sixto Martínez
Avda. Madrid, 14.
✆ *958 271 323.*
Great variety of scientific magazines and books. Specialised in health sciences.

Melgamúsic
Pedro Antonio de Alarcón, 5.
✆ *958 253 059.*
Rock and Blues.

Discocinta
Nueva de San Antón, 9.
✆ *958 251 314.*
Novelties and classics at good prices.

Numismatics, philately, etc.

Puerta Real
Acera del Casino, 15.
✆ *958 222 472.*

El Galeón
Verónica de la Magdalena, 25.
✆ *958 267 165.*

Fashion

As well as the department stores and national firms like Cortefiel, Roberto Verino, Adolfo Dominguez, Loewe, etc., there are many other quality shops.

Shopping in Granada

At night, the old streets of Granada become spontaneous baazars.

- **Unisex:**

VOGUE
Ganivet, 14.
Quality, distinctive clothing.

EMA
Sierpe Baja, 4.
Any style at affordable prices.

PINILLAS
San Antón, 18.
Clothes for young ones, good taste and opportunities.

- **Men's fashion:**

LATINO
Obispo Hurtado, 11.
Wide offer in quality suits.

JOTA
Milagro, 1.
Elegance today. Assorted ties.

ÁNGEL
Reyes Católicos, 2.
Good style in a reduce space.

CAMISEROS ARTESANOS
Montería, 2.
Made-to-measure shirts.

- **Women's fashion:**

CANDELA
Mesones, 7.
Novelties for all the tastes.

PUPUS
Montería, s/n.
Excellent variety and imagination.

DELY'S
Moras, s/n (with Almona del Campillo).
Very exclusive.

- **Other clothing:**

ZERIMAR
Carretera de Málaga, s/n (Santa Fe).
Leather garments.

Shopping in Granada

ESTRELLA SÁNCHEZ
Horno de Abad, 13.
Flamenco dresses.

EL ROCÍO
Pasaje Conde Alcalá, s/n.
Flamenco dresses.

Antiques

The most recognized area for antique dealers in Granada is Elvira Street.

FERNÁNDEZ CAMPOS
Elvira, 40. ✆ *958 224 667*

J. REYES MUÑOZ
Elvira, 5. ✆ *958 207 608*

PRIOR TEMPORE
Elvira, 100. ✆ *958 204 608*

Buying rare goods is also possible in many other places.

ALMONEDA SAGITARIO
Ramón y Cajal, 1. ✆ *958 267 822*

ANTAÑO
Virgen de la Capilla, 7.
✆ *958 253 735*

L. RUIZ LINARES
Zacatín, 21. ✆ *958 222 347*

Gifts, decorative items...

As well as handicrafts, pottery and traditional items, its is also possible to buy prestige gifts at reduced prices with no harm to quality.

VIANCA
Obispo Hurtado, 11.
Any price.

LINDE
Reyes Católicos, 21.
Speciality in glass and china.

LA OCA
San Antón, 36.
Casual and juvenile presents for an easy-going decoration.

Flowers

In Granada, they are bought in any of the well-provided typical street stalls at the Bib Rambla Square, where buying flowers is almost a spectacle.

Sport

Obviously, due to the vicinity of the Sierra Nevada, there is a wide variety of ski equipment, but it is also easy to find gymnastic accessories, mountaineering garments, etc.

DEPORTES NEVADA
Ángel Ganivet, 15. ✆ *958 222 051*

STRINTER
Carretera de Armilla, s/n.
The hypermarket of sport.

LA IMPERIAL
Mesones Street.
An varied stock in the city centre.

Anywhere is good for walking and shopping in Granada.

Shopping in Granada

Shopping in Granada

Typical souvenir shop.

Nightlife

The nightlife of Granada is famous even beyond the Spanish borders. Mani guiris (foreigners) look for the movida (nightlife) area, located in the streets of Pedro Antonio de Alarcón, Emperatriz Eugenia, Gonzalo Gallas and the surrounding areas. Another very hectic zone is the Plaza Nueva, the first part of Elvira Street and the raise to the Albaicin by Calderería Street.
In the summertime, the atmosphere is at the Paseo de los Tristes (Promenade of the Sad Ones), a contradictory name for such and exciting and loud area. This peculiar name is an inheritance from the time when this was the road to the old cemetery, where the funerals came and went in processions of sad faces. Very different from the present reality.

CULTURE LIFE AND SHOWS

UNIVERSITY OF GRANADA
Hospital Real, s/n. ✆ 958 243 000.
Vice-rectorate for University Activities: ✆ *958 243 014.* It has a theatre group, an exhibit hall, a library, film club and the most ample variety of cultural services It publishes several free magazines and newspapers, where the events of the

university cultural seasons are listed in detail.

Obra Social de La General
Reyes Católicos, 51.
📞 958 244 596.
It organises exhibits, concerts of ancient and contemporary music, etc.

Cultura de la Diputación
Palacio de los Condes de Gabia, s/n.
📞 958 247 371.
Its famous exhibits of contemporary art and photography stand up among its multiple cultural activities.

There is thorough information about the daily activities organized by the public and private institutions in the cultural pages of Granada's single local newspaper, placed at the end. www.ideal.es
The Junta de Andalucía (autonomous government of Andalusia) publishes a Leisure Guide in different languages. This monthly magazine is called *¿Qué hacer? / What's on?* and is available at the tourism offices.

Cinemas

Average price 4 € On Wednesday –except for bank holidays– the price is lower (2,5 €) and sesión golfa (naughty pass) at discounted prices after midnight.

Cine Aliatar (3 screens)
Recogidas, 2. 📞 958 261 984.
purl.ocic.org/net/aliatar/

University film club
Main Lecture Hall of the Faculty of Science. 📞 958 243 000.
It is held during the school year, once or twice a week, with high quality seasons, revival, monographic programs, old movies, etc. Affordable prices.

Granada, 10
Cárcel Baja, 10. 📞 958 256 640.
This cinema has club seats, as it actually becomes a club at midnight.

Madrigal
Carrera del Genil, 14-16.
📞 958 224 348.
Almost a Granadine institutions. Spacious room and big screen.

Multicines Centro (8 screens)
Solarillo de Gracia, 9. 📞 958 252 996

Neptuno Multicines (8 screens)
Neptuno Shopping Centre
📞 958 520 412 / 958 520 407.
www.multicines-neptuno.com
Movies for all tastes.

Alhambra multicines
CC Alcampo. Ctra. Jaén, s/n.
www.cineciudad.com

Theatres and auditoriums

In Granada, classic music concerts, opera, theatre, conferences, etc. are almost continuous. Normally the season starts in September and climaxes in the celebrations of the Corpus Christi. There is a municipal box office in Acera del Casino, outside the Isabel la Católica Theatre, where, as well as tickets, visitors may obtain information about all the music and theatre events scheduled in Granada.
The premises where these evening and night events are held are:

Nightlife

In the modern premises of the Palacio de Exposiciones y Congresos (congress centre) converge a fair share of the cultural life of Granada.

Auditórium of the Manuel de Falla Cultural Centre
Paseo de los Mártires, s/n.
☏ 958 229 681.
The acoustic quality of this hall is famous. Its program includes full seasons of symphonic and chamber concerts, with international soloists or ensembles; together with the concerts of the Granada City Orchestra. Thus, there are usually two or more concerts per week. Prices range from 6 € to 18 € Season tickets and discount tikets for students and other collectives available.

Palacio de Exposiciones y Congresos (Congress Centre)
Paseo del Violón, s/n. ☏ 958 127 747.
Occasional opera plays, concerts and performances for the "general public". Prices range from 9 € to 15 € Club and season discount tickets.

Alhambra Theatre
Molinos, 56. ☏ 958 220 447.
Small stalls, but large stage. Andalusian companies and contemporary creations. Interesting morning passes for school kids.

Municipal Theatre Isabel la Católica
Acera del Casino, s/n. Telephone box office: ☏ 902 400 222.
A lifelong establishment that offers the national hits touring the country.

Exhibit halls

Xauen
Pedro Antonio de Alarcón, 18.
☏ 958 254 835

Casa de los Tiros
Pl. Padre Suárez, 17. ☏ 958 223 412.
Exhibits sponsored by the Junta de Andalucía.

Centro Gran Capitán
Gran Capitán, 22. ☏ 958 201 372.
Exhibits sponsored by the Granada City Council.

Nightlife

CASA DE PORRAS
Albaicín. ✆ 958 243 484

CORRALA DE SANTIAGO
Realejo. ✆ 958 220 527.
Exhibits sponsored by the University of Granada.

CENTRO DE LA GENERAL
Acera del Casino, 9. ✆ 958 227 791.
Very interesting retrospective and historic exhibits.

MUSEUM-HOUSE OF GARCÍA LORCA.
Fuentevaqueros. ✆ 958 516 453.
Exhibits about Federico García Lorca.

Live music clubs

PUB ESHAVIRA
Cuna Street, 2 (next to Elvira).
✆ 958 290 829.
Hidden club with great live jazz and flamenco.

INDUSTRIAL COPERA
Ctra. Armilla. C/ La Paz, nave 7.
Main figures, high level rock concerts and DJ sessions.

EL SECADERO
Antigua Carretera de la Costa, 53 (Alhendín). ✆ 958 558 039.
A must-go for jazz lovers. Unusual background.

ALEXIS VIERNES
Atarfe-Santa Fe Road, km 1.
✆ 958 440 226.
Jazz, blues and South American music for the weekend.

HARÉN DE ARQUÍMEDES
Sol, 13.
Singer-songwriter music.

Tablaos flamencos

LOS TARANTOS
Camino del Sacromonte, 9.
✆ 958 224 525 / 958 222 492.
Quality Gipsy zambras in the heart of the Sacromonte.

EL CAMBORIO
Camino del Sacromonte, s/n.
✆ 958 221 215.
Club atmosphere in the flamenco quarter.

VENTA EL GALLO
Barranco de los Negros, 5. (Sacromonte).

EL CORRAL DEL PRÍNCIPE
Campo de Príncipe, s/n.
✆ 958 228 088.
Also traditional Granadine restaurant.

JARDINES NEPTUNO
Arabial, s/n.
✆ 958 252 050 / 958 251 112.
Dance hall with flamenco shows.

REINA MORA
Mirador de San Cristóbal. Road to Murcia. ✆ 958 273 228

ZAMBRA DE MARÍA LA CANASTERA
Sacromonte, 89. ✆ 958 121 193 / 907 578 751.

Bingo halls and casinos

SAN ANTÓN
San Antón, 4. ✆ 958 258 406

LA PLATERÍA
Acera de Darro. 16-18.
✆ 958 250 697.

Clubs

GRANADA, 10
Cárcel Baja, 10.
✆ 958 224 001/
958 224 126.
Former theatre with very high ceilings transformed into a vast cinema and club.

Nightlife

DISTRITO 10
Gran Capitán, 5. ℘ 958 280 290.
The club in the centre of the movida.

FLEMING
Dr. Guirao, s/n. ℘ 958 283 391.
Smart club near the Faculty of Medicine.

MEETING POINT
Plaza de Gracia, s/n.
Very young atmosphere.

PALACIO DE LA MÚSICA
Arabial, 162. ℘ 958 277 421.
Young atmosphere near the trendy area.

DRINK BARS AND TRENDY AREAS

The busiest areas, especially during the weekend, are Pedro Antonio de Alarcón and Plaza Nueva. There are also big gatherings of young people around the clubs and cinemas of the Plaza de Gracia. A more quiet atmosphere can be enjoyed at the Campo del Príncipe, in the Realejo. Unless in cold winter days, the squares ot the Albaicin, especially Aliatar, San Miguel Bajo and San Nicolás, are very busy and there are always some terraces to have a tapa or a ración.

Plaza Nueva and Paseo de los Tristes

PILAR DEL TORO
Next to Saint Anne Church.
A lordly courtyard of the XVIIth century transformed into an excellent place for chatting. All along the Carrera de Darro, there are night bars with the most diverse atmospheres. Take a look before going in, in order to choose the best for your style.

Enjoy the purest flamenco of the city at the caves of the Sacromonte.

Terrace near the river Darro, under the attentive and always present gaze of the Alhambra.

La Fuente
Traditional bar of the Paseo de los Tristes with a big terrace in front of the Alhambra in summer nights. The adjacent bars, very similar to it, are also good for a drink in an unparalleled background. Cosmopolitan atmosphere.

Aljibe
*Ánimas Street
(near Cuchilleros Saquare).*
Casual and young atmosphere.

La Fontana
Carrera de Darro, s/n.
For a drink at the foot of the Alhambra.

Albaicin area

Casa Yanguas
Near Aliatar Square (Albaicín).
An unusual place for a drink: a Morisco house that welcomes night-birds and sometimes offers contemporary art exhibits.

Tea houses at Caldereria Street
Lower Albaicín.
An unprecedented and very recent aspect of the Albaicin is the opening of oriental-style tea houses. Most of them are at Calderedía Street and surroundings, and add an exotic

Nightlife

Oriental bars and restaurants fill the streets of the old quarter with exoticism.

note with a pretended historical legitimacy to the Arab quarter. They lead a peaceful coexistence with the traditional and typical establishments of the Albaicin.

Despite most of them are very narrow, they are excellent for a calm afternoon snack with Arab sweets or just to spend a quiet time over a mint tea. There are diverse flavours for diverse tastes.

Peña La Platería
Placeta Toqueros, 7 (Albaicín).
✆ *958 227 712.*

Nightlife

A must for flamenco lovers. Inside covered with flamenco souvenirs and pictures. Outdoors terrace, ideal for summer nights and Sunday mornings. The bar serves Granadine dishes.

City centre

BIB RAMBLA SQUARE
In this time-honoured square, there are several terraces where the famous hot chocolate with churros can be tasted when musical evenings are held in Granada, especially after the concerts of the International Festival of Music and Dance. They also serve bocatas (French bread sandwiches) and sandwiches, and even a light dinner, if necessary.

LA YEDRA
Molinos Street.
This beautiful sloped terrace opens only in summer and is a very good choice for its views and environment.

PAPALAGI
C/ Capitanía, s/n.
Imaginative cocktails.

BRITANIA, PORTOLANO AND RINASCIMENTO
Three very smart drink bars located next to each other in the centre of Alhamar Street.

University area

LA BODEGA INGLESA
Albert Einstein Square, 14.
A smart bar very close to the Science University Campus.

EL BORRACHO DE ORO
Martínez de la Rosa, 10.
A very diverse atmosphere.

BOULEVARD
Guirao Gea, 2.
A discreet drink bar next to the Faculty of Medicine.

LA TERTULIA
Pintor López Mezquita, 3.
Literary atmosphere, tango, soft music, theatre and other cultural activities.

The city of Granada has a wide variety of fun environments.

Festivities in Granada

DEEP ROOTED CUSTOMS AND TRADITIONS

There are many fiestas, fairs and contests in Granada during the year. The religious and lay aspects mix in the deepest-rooted Granadine customs and traditions. The following is a selection of the most relevant ones:

La fiesta de la Toma (January 2)

On January 2 of 1492, Muhammad XII Abu 'Abd Allah, the last king of Granada, delivered the keys of the city to the Catholic Monarchs, Ferdinand II of Aragon and Isabella I of Castile. That event –immortalized by the painter Pradilla– is the origin of this fiesta called "de la toma" (of the conquest), despite new names –like Fiesta of Tolerance, or Fiesta of the Three Cultures– have emerged in the last years. In that day, Muhammad XII Abu 'Abd Allah surrendered his sword to the Christians and left in direction to the Alpujarras. The legend reads that the king started crying when the city went out of sight, and then his mother said: "Cry like a woman over what you could not defend like a man". In the meanwhile, the

Festivities in Granada

Catholic Monarchs hoisted the banner of Castile in the highest tip of the Alhambra. That sword of Muhammad XII Abu 'Abd Allah (actually, one of his two swords, as the other is kept in the Museum of the Army in Madrid) and that banner of Castile march in the civic-religious procession celebrated this day. After the solemn mass in the Royal Chapel, before the graves of the Catholic Monarchs, the ceremonial aedile hoists the banner to which military honours are granted. At noon, the religious-civic procession leaves this royal temple with the sword and the banner to take them to the City Hall, where they are exhibited. There, the aedile hoists the banner again, this time at the main balcony of the Hall, while calling the city with the sentence *"Granada..., Granada..., Granada... por los ínclitos reyes Isabel y Fernando"* (for the illustrious monarchs Isabella and Ferdinand).

All day long, the Campana de la Vela (Bell of the Candle), located at the namesake tower of the Alhambra, where the Castilian banner hoisted on the day of the conquer, rings. The tradition says that the girls who touch the bell in that day will marry during that year.

San Cecilio popular pilgrimage (February 1)

There is an old legend that says the Apostolic Barons, direct disciples of the Apostles came to evangelise Spain. Among them was Saint Cecil *(San Cecilio),* who was the first bishop of Granada, and died under torture in the outskirts of the city, in the hill of Valparaiso, that from then on was called the Sacromonte. By the end of the XVIth century, some human bones were found in that place and were thought to be the relic of the saint. A great popular pilgrimage to the Sacromonte is celebrated in early February in memory of that finding.

In order to have a more relaxed celebration and to allow as much people as possible to participate, the liturgy, the *Mozarabe* mass and the visit to the holy caves, where the torture was supposed to happen, are celebrated on the 1st. And the following Sunday, the pilgrimage honouring the

All the festive celebrations in Granada have a manifest popular flavour.

111

Festivities in Granada

> **Note**
>
> There are also meetings, festivals and contests with no fixed date. Some of the most relevant are the Festival of Ancient Music, the Festival of Contemporary Music, the Contest of Cinema "Young Producers", Organ Season, etc.

patron of the city is done, together with regional dancing at the flat areas of the hill, an excursion to the *siete cuestas* (seven slopes), etc. During the picnic, the City Council offers the pilgrims a tasting of the first broad beans of the season, served with cod and *jayuyas,* small oil bread pancakes with coarse salt. Also, the wineskins of the first wine of the season, the famous *costa,* are open in that day.

The Albaicin, located in the neighbouring hill, celebrates a similar pilgrimage on September 29. The pilgrims walk up to the Hermitage of San Miguel el Alto, in the *Cerro del Aceituno,* where the panoramic views are impressive.

Spring celebration (March 24/25)

In this still young celebration, the city welcomes the spring. The City Council sponsors cultural itineraries across the city, guided tours to monuments, exhibits and poets. There are concerts, *flamenco* shows, street theatre, games, nightly amusements and street parties. The activities are held in the Paseo de los Tristes and the flat area of the Congress Centre.

Easter

Granadine Easter is among the most emotive and bright in Spain. It was originated by the Counter-Reformation and the new liturgical doctrines that preached a closer approach of the people to the details of the Passion of Christ. Soon, the Baroque spirit started expressing all these feelings in theatre plays and took them to every corner of the city. This is how brotherhoods started the processions of their worshipped and magnificent images. Granadine Easter starts on the afternoon of Palm Sunday, when *La Borriquilla* (the little donkey) goes to the penitence station of the brotherhoods of the *Resucitado* that are confined on the Easter Sunday night. Unlike in Castile, the Andalusian Easter is extrovert and brimming with decorative and ornamental magnificence. It is also important to remember the importance of the sculptural value of the images, most of which are master pieces of the Granadine school of *imaginería* (carving of images), dating from the XVIth to XVIII centuries. The richness of the *tronos* (heavy religious floats), carved in noble woods and covered with silver or copper and flowers must not be forgotten. The canopies and gowns of the Virgins rival in rich embroidery. Each procession has a particular flavour, an identificative Coat-of-Arms and many other peculiarities that visitors have to discover. Do not forget to reach for the best place to see them march. It is advisable to go to the Cathedral gate every night, where all the processions need to go in order to observe the ancient rite of penitence. But if you wish to discover the charm of a *paso de palio* in a typical street or a Christ framed in an unequalled background, get ready to move around the old town and the historical quarters. The following are some of the best places: the exit of the Universitaria; the Campo del Príncipe to see Los Favores; the cuesta de Alhacaba and the pasajes of San Gregorio for La Aurora; the carrera de Darro, at the foot of the Alhambra, for El Silencio; the cuesta del Chapiz and the raises to Sacromonte to see Los Gitanos; Cárcel Street for La Cañilla; San Antón for the Cristo de San Agustín; the Arco de la Justicia, at the Alhambra, for Sta María de la Alhambra, etc. From any corner or any balcony may come out a *saeta*, a traditional *cante* freed to the night with a particular style and full of feelings.

The day of the Cross (May 3)

One of the most traditional Granadine celebrations. The Christian celebration in honour of the Holy Cross merges with

Colour, sevillanas *and folklore are always part of the celebrations.*

the pagan celebration of May, very popular among ancient Romans. This is basically a street celebration that starts on the day before. In squares and courtyards of the historical quarters and the Albaicin, Granadine people put crosses covered with carnations and decorated with any possible item: plant pots, copper and pottery decorations, guitars, traditional articles, forged iron pots, Manila shawls, diverse handicrafts... Two elements cannot be forgotten: a *pero* (a flaw) and some scissors, so that visitors can cut out any flaw, in case they think the cross has one. At the foot of the crosses, there are *tablaos* for *sevillanas* and other traditional dances, and a bar for refreshing the throats. The visit to the crosses lasts all day, and locals usually wear regional costumes and a carnation in their hair or in a buttonhole. Of course, there is also plenty chatting with friends and cross-judgments while having the traditional *tapas* with *fino*. The awards of the cross contest are delivered that very evening.

The Corpus Christi

These are the most important fiestas and fairs of Granada. Its tradition comes from the time when the Catholic Monarchs granted a fair on the Corpus Christi celebration day to the recently conquered city. It was established by Pope Urban IV in the early XIVth century. The main celebration is held on the Thursday following the eight Sunday after Easter Sunday. In Granada, the celebration start on Wednesday with the pagan procession of the *Tarasca*, a dragon carrying a young girls dressed according to the fashion of that year. The woman stepping on the roaring dragon is accompanied by a retinue of *gigantes* and *cabezudos* (giant and big-headed figures) who provoke the people and play with them. The name of *Tarasca* seems to come from the French region of La Tarasque, where Saint Martha dominated a dragon that was terrorizing the region. In the procession, there are also municipal macebearers dressed in antique clothing. The religious procession is on Thursday, with the artistic Granadine monstrance that leaves the Cathedral at noon.

The streets are full of sedge, *mastranzo* and *gayomba* and other aromatic plants while rose petals fall from the balconies as the Eucharist passes. There are embellished altars along the route. There are cattle fairs in the outskirts, and in Bib Rambla, visitors may find traditional *carocas*, posters with caricatures and verses making fun of the city life. There are *casetas* for amusement, dancing and *tapeo* at the Real de la Feria. Also, during the entire week, there are bullfights, street parties and popular fiestas in different quarters, rides for children, sporting contests, exhibitions, etc.

Fiesta de la música (Celebration of Music)

Since a few years ago, the Granada City Orchestra inaugurates its music season with great open-air concerts spiced with festive entertainments, fireworks, multimedia shows, etc. This celebration, held on the flat area outside the Congress Centre, starts after the sunset on the first week of September.

New Year's Eve

Like many other cities, Granada says goodbye to the year with a great celebration at the Plaza del Carmen, in front of the City Hall, which is frequently broadcasted on TV. The City Council distributes free grapes and cava.

Flamenco is so deep-rooted that even stones succumb.

FAIRS AND CONTESTS

Fiesta of the Patron Virgin and fair of autumn fruits

Despite the canonical commemoration of the festivity of the *Virgen de las Angustias* (Virgin of the Anguish), Patron Virgin of Granada, is on September 15, the popular celebration is held on the last Sunday of that month. There are continuous formal events offered by the different associations of the city that culminate on the 15th with an impressive floral offering before the façade of the basilica.
The traditional fair of autumn fruits, with exhibit and sale of products of the province is held in *La Carrera* during the last weekend of September. On the dawn of Sunday, the image of the Virgin is taken from the basilica to the Cathedral during the Morning Rosary, and in the evening a solemn procession culminates the celebrations.

Book fairs

Several book fairs are held in Granada, either at the *Puerta Real* or in the nearby palaces. Local booksellers present the new publications at discounted prices in the street fair of April 23.
Feria general de muestras (Trade Fair)

It is held during the last week of September at the premises of Santa Juliana, outside Granada on the way to Armilla. The most innovative business and trade projects are presented there.

Granada
for children

The gardens of Granada are well known and widely admired. The most remarkable are those of the Generalife and the Alhambra. They are undoubtedly the most luxurious, the most visited and the most pictured, but in most cases, the visit involves only admiring them on the rush to see the sights. However, there is a small wood surrounding the walls of the Alhambra where visitors can go for quiet walks, reading or chatting. Being in a small and steep area, it is not well conditioned for children. It is rather a leisure and sport area for grown-ups.

GARDENS FOR FAMILY WALKS

García Lorca Park

Already mentioned in the historical routes. It is large and well looked after and has all kinds of facilities and services for children: swings, slides, webs, wooden ships, seesaws, fountains, etc. For grown-ups there is a bar, a terrace, etc.
Its interest as a garden is high, actually one of the highest in Granada: it has typical plants of the entire Mediterranean environment, myrtle hedges and the best rose garden in Southern Spain, with more

Granada for children

than one hundred different roses.

Genil Gardens

Located along the right bank of river Genil, before it receives the Darro. It is a wooden stretch of land, with *tierra de albero* (bullring sand). Its design makes it more suitable for walking than for a long stay with children.

Fuentenueva Park

It is around the Faculty of Science. The woodland is thick, with plentiful shades. There are premises for skating, walking, stretching, etc. There are also winding paths, grass, benches, etc. The university sporting facilities are next to the park and can be used both by children and grown-ups.

OTHER GARDENS AND SMALL PARKS

They can be found here and there across the different quarters of Granda (Triunfo, Vergeles, Chana, etc.). There are temporary mini parks with swings and many other rides for children, in different areas of Granada. For example, the rides at the entrance of Neptuno Shopping Centre are very popular with children.

PLAYING AND LEARNING

SCIENCE PARK

The facilities are suitable for any age, but pay special attention to children. There is a marquee where the youngest ones will take a guided approach to the science, while playing. Little ones and adults will enjoy the interactive Museum where the motto is "Do Touch".

The García Lorca Park, embracing the Huerta de San Vicente, is the perfect environment for elders to relax and a safe place for children to play.

Granada for children

Walking around the gardens of Granada, you can be near the generous nature without renouncing the pleasures of the city.

Theatre for children
Alhambra Theatre
✆ 902 118 521 985 226 462.
A proposal for a children theatre season to be developed during the school year. The name of this experience is *abecedaria* and gives kids the opportunity to enjoy the best theatre companies for children, and also the chance to attend debates about the plays, writing and painting workshops or to take an active part the plays.

Happy Swing
Children play centre. Pedro Antonio de Alarcón, s/n. ✆ 958 521 099.
All kinds of plays, interior plastic parks, carpet picnics with friends, celebrations and more.

Amusement arcade
Eurosalón 2002
Acera de Darro, 30. Pagés, 1 (Albaicín).
Avda. Dílar, 22.
Speciality in all kinds of game machines.

Neptuno Shopping Centre
It has many amusement establishments, from the traditional table football to the most modern electronic and computing games.

Huerto Alegre Farm School
Ctra. de Almuñécar, km 27 (Albuñuelas). ✆ 958 793 262.
Nature's classroom.

Children library
Profesor Sáinz Cantero, 6-ground floor.
✆ 958 805 038

TOYS AND TEACHING MATERIAL

Luden
Acera de Darro, 92.
✆ 958 250 402.
Everything in traditional and didactic toys.

Dencina
San Juan de Dios, s/n.
✆ 958 465 084.
Polychromatic wooden toys.

HAMBURGER AND PIZZA BARS

The food of other places can be found in Granada, too.

McDonald's
Recogidas, 18. ℘ 958 264 140.
As anywhere else, this famous establishment offers its well-known products in afternoon snacks, dinners with friends, etc. Special clown shows some days of the week.

Pizza Hut
Avda. Constitución, 9. ℘ 958 277 512

Telepizza
Gran Vía, 40. Acera de Darro, 80.
Avda. Madrid, 23. Next to Sporting Palace.
℘ 958 255 432

Burguer King
Neptuno Shopping Centre, 2ⁿᵈ floor.
℘ 958 521 765

Ídolos & Fans
Camino Ronda, 80. ℘ 958 536 022

Pizza World
Emperatriz Eugenia, 9-11.
℘ 958 206 262

ICE-CREAM PARLOUR

Los Italianos
Gran Vía, 4. ℘ 958 224 034

Nevada
Carrera del Genil, 17. ℘ 958 225 200

Isla
Carrera del Genil, 27.
℘ 958 222 405

ATTRACTIONS AND AMUSEMENTS

Diverama. Recreational activities
Músico Ayala Cantó, 4.
℘ 958 262 676

Attrezo
Baleares, 7 (Monachil).
℘ 958 301 068.
Children parties, theatre, juggling, magic, etc.

Parks in the outskirts

As well as the parks that are occasionally installed for fairs, in the outskirts of Granada, we can find:

Aquaola
Ctra. de la Sierra, km 4 (Cenes de la Vega).
℘ 958 486189 /
958 489 132.
Aquatic and theme park in the valley of the Genil. It has a restaurant and several services for children and grown ups. Open in the summer season. Regular bus service from Granada.

Ermita de los Tres Juanes
(Hermitage of the Three Johns)
Sierra Elvira (near the village of Atarfe). Amazing panoramic views. Children and grown ups will enjoy the collections of minerals and fossils, living animals, indigenous plants, etc.

SPORTING PREMISES

Swimming pools

NEPTUNO
Arabial, s/n. ℘ 958 251 055

MIAMI
Camino Purchil, s/n. ℘ 958 250 031

BAHÍA
Camino Neveros, 73 (Huétor Vega). ℘ 958 500 601

Skating and similar

SNOWBOARD
Casillas de Prats, 5. ℘ 958 254 558

RADA
Pl. Andalucía, local 6 (Sierra Nevada). ℘ 958 480 753

Cycling, bike rental, routes, etc.

The nature around Granada invites for these rides.

SEMAR
San Juan de Dios, 48. ℘ 958 278 072

SPORT CENTRES

Sport practicing and attending as viewer.

"GRANADA 74" SPORT CLUB
Avda. Pulianas, s/n. ℘ 958 202 505/ 958 154 693

ESTADIO DE LA JUVENTUD (YOUTH STADIUM)
Ronda, 171. ℘ 958 291 224

MONTALBÁN – TANDEM GRANADA SCHOOL
Conde Cifuentes, 11. ℘ 958 256 875

LOS CÁRMENES NEW STADIUM
Zaidín, s/n.
Famous and renowned stadium where sometimes the Spanish National Football Team plays.

CITY SPORTING PALACE PINTOR MALDONADO
Camino de la Zubia, s/n (Zaidín). ℘ 958 130 829

MOTRIL CITY SPORT CENTRE
Camino Cerro del Toro (Motril).
Athletics court.

Ice-cream parlour in the city centre.

FLYING AND PARAGLIDING

Alfaguara Flight Club
Nogales, s/n. Urb. Las Fncinas (Alfacar). ℘ *958 543 259*

Elibirge Flight Club
Avda. Alfaguara, 152 (Alfacar).

Paragliding club
Alfredo Velasco, 8-3º F (Almuñécar).
℘ *958 532 159*

"Draco" Free Flight Club
Avda. Coronel Muñoz, 108.
℘ *958 280 608*

"Granada" Free Flight Club
Santa Fe, 3-ground floor.
℘ *958 222 103*

"Velasur" Flight Club
Oidores, 15 (Granada). ℘ *958 222 103*

"Motril" Andalusian Sporting School of Paragliding
Santísimo, 28 (Motril). ℘ *958 822 759*

WATER AND SEA SPORTS

"Punta de la Mona" Marina
Urbanización Marina de Este (Almuñécar). ℘ *958 827 018*

"El Puerto" Marina
Motril. ℘ *958 600 037*

Acuaola
Cenes de la Vega (5 km from Granada). ℘ *958 486 189.*

Aquapark, mainly for youth.

La Herradura Windsurf
Promenade (Paseo Marítimo), *Las Olas building* (La Herradura). ℘ *958 640 143*

SKI AND MOUNTAIN SPORTS

The proximity of the Sierra Nevada is a good spur for the practice of these sports.

High Performance Sport Centre in Sierra Nevada
Pradollano, s/n (Sierra Nevada).
℘ *958 480 722*

Pradollano Ski Resort
Sierra Nevada. ℘ *958 249 100.*
Informs on the organization of children initiation to ski.

TENNIS, GOLF, RIDING...

Granada Royal Tennis Society
Camino Conejeras, El Serrallo.
℘ *958 123 311*

Granada Royal Riding Society
Ctra. de la Zubia, s/n. ℘ *958 811 006*

Los Moriscos Golf Club
Urbanización Playa Granada (Motril).
℘ *958 825 527*

Granada Golf Club
Avda. Los Corsarios, s/n (Las Gabias).
℘ *958 584 436*

Royal Trapshooting Society
Embalse Cubillas, Albolote. Ctra. Jaén, km 115. ℘ *958 499 058*

Multi Ocio Children and youth camps
Pescadería, 1-1º. ℘ *958 262 414*
Recommended for formative camps, nature sports and small adventures in the province.

Granada for children

Granada for children

Children playground. García Lorca Park.

Outings in the surrounding areas

The province of Granada is an universe of beautiful contrasts opening before the eyes of visitors to deliver a full range of feelings that will wake their senses up.
Everything oozes with a powerful magnetism that makes visitors want to always come back to this land: the historical routes that bring together the present and the most glorious and important pasts of Spain, the extremely beautiful natural spots, the evoking Mediterranean beaches, or the traces left by poets and artists.

EXCURSION I: BORDER PLACES

The north and the west of the province was the border between the Christian and Muslim kingdoms for a long time. The remains of that strain are several walled villages and castles scattered across the province.
Heading north, the villages of **Iznalloz** and **Píñar.** Pay attention to its traditionally Andalusian nucleus of houses with a castle. In Píñar, the castle crowns a hill inside which a cave with interesting archaeological and paleontological deposits was found.

Outings in the surrounding areas

On the northwest, the most important defensive castle is that of **Alcalá la Real,** a village in Jaen, but very fond of Granada. Its castle is called *Fortaleza de la Mota* (Fortress of the Mota) and also houses a former abbey with Gothic plan. Closer to Granada, we find **Moclín,** with another interesting castle that is being restored at the moment. The view from its top embraces almost half Andalusia. Here and there, we also find watchtowers that linked and transmitted the signals of the fortress.

On the west, the key town is **Loja:** located by the river Genil, in the strategic crossing point, not far from the fantastic *Infiernos* (hell). As well as the Arab-originated Alcazaba, Loja is proud of its Renaissance Church of Saint Gabriel, the Neo-classic Church of the *Encarnación* and the mausoleum of General Narváez...

On the southwest, the key locality was **Alhama,** whose capture was cried in ballads. Its location over a huge cliff made it did without a conspicuous castle. Yet, the military function of the city can be perceived in its parish church. The cliffs, the Baroque Church of the *Carmen,* and the *pósito* (an institution that lent grain to poor peasants in harsh times) are also worth visiting.

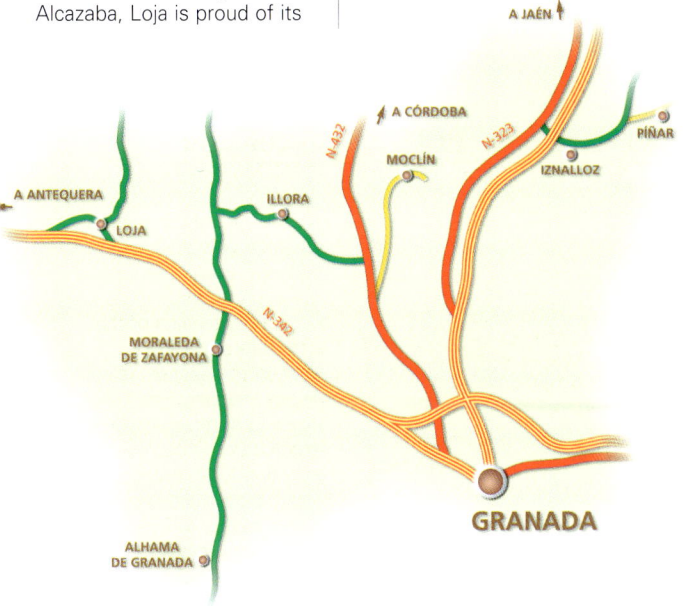

Outings in the surrounding areas

Moclín castle and enclosure.

EXCURSION II: THE CONQUER OF GRANADA

The final stage of the Conquer of Granada was carried out from a camp that the Catholic Monarchs set in the river plain, almost at the gates of Granada. This camp later became the current village of Santa Fe.

Santa Fe is some 10 km from Granada and has a very peculiar Greek cross-shaped town planning, with a monumental gate at the end of each of the four sides. At the centre of the cross, created by the two main streets of the village, there is the square, the elegant neo-classic church, the town hall, with hints of Mudejar style, and the former *Casa* Real (Royal House). Also, Santa Fe has de epithet of Cradle of Spanishness, as it was in the building next to its church where the capitulations between the Catholic Monarchs and Columbus were signed, enabling the Admiral to begin his trips. There are several reminders of those capitulations all around the village. Do not forget to try some of the good products of the river valley and the traditional sweets called *piononos*. A few miles away there is another famous place linked to Columbus, **Pinos Puente,** where the royal heralds met a heavy-hearted Columbus, who was leaving Granada after the refusal of the queen to finance his trip, and told him that she had changed her mind.

There are other places linked to the conquest and worth visiting. The legend says that Isabella the Catholic was once almost captured by the Moors in **La Zubia,** where she planted a laurel. **Atarfe** lays at the foot of Sierra Elvira, the closest hill to Granada, from which the Alhambra with the

Outings in the surrounding areas

The spot known as "El suspiro del Moro" (The moor's sigh) is a magic enclave from which splendid views of Granada and the Sierra Nevada can be seen.

Outings in the surrounding areas

The surrender of Granada. Canvas of F. Pradilla conserved in the Palacio del Senado *(Senate Palace), in Madrid.*

background of the Sierra Nevada is clearly seen. There is also a hermitage dedicated to *Los Tres Juanes* (The Three Johns).
Last, but not least, the **Suspiro del Moro** (The Moor's Sigh) must be mentioned. The tradition says that it was in this port, separating the Atlantic and the Mediterranean waters, where the last king of Granada, Muhammad XII Abu 'Abd Allah, saw for the last time the city he had lost. Hearing him sigh, his mother Aisha, pronounced the famous words: "Cry like a woman over what you could not defend like a man".

EXCURSION III: AFTER THE TRAIL OF LORCA

This excursion would take visitors to places related to the life and death of Federico García Lorca (1898-1936). The *Huerta de San Vicente* and other places related to the poet have been already visited in the city. Leave Granada by the A-92, dual carriageway to Seville and Malaga, ant take the exit to **Fuentevaqueros** (some 10 km away). The poet's native home is in this mainly agricultural hamlet of the river plain. It now houses a small and charming museum with items and souvenirs of the poet, and exhibit room, a courtyard for talks and poem readings, etc. Visitors are received with great care.
Near Fuentevaqueros, it is worth visiting the small village of **Valderrubio,** a place that Lorca

Outings in the surrounding areas

mentioned in several poems and of which was very fond.
While doing this route, take the chance to admire the shire of *Vega de Granada,* a plain with particular geographic and anthropologic interest by the river Genil. Do not miss the the crops from the vegetable gardens, the vast poplar groves, the tobacco and the

García Lorca Park.

unparalleled brick or wooden drying sheds.
Back to the A-92, heading to Murcia, drive along Granada and take the exit to **Alfacar.** Above the village, in the way from Fuente Grande to Víznar, there are the crags where many Granadine people were killed during the Civil War. A park in remembrance of the death of Lorca has been created in one of them.

EXCURSION IV: NATIONAL PARK OF SIERRA DE HUÉTOR

This excursion begins were the last one ends.

Fuentegrande, a spectacular open-air carstic upwelling, is near the García Lorca Park in Víznar-Alfacar The Aidanamar irrigation ditch, which has supplied Granada with fresh and clean water since the Arab times, begins there. A must see in **Víznar** is the Archbishop's Palace. The Natural Park, 10 km far from Granada, begins a bit further. The **Sierra de la Alfaguara** is a better known and more accessible place. Also, it has highland nature enclaves with conditioned hiking areas. There is a **Natural Park of Sierra de Huétor** interpretation centre, as well as camping and leisure areas, fountains, etc.

Outings in the surrounding areas

EXCURSION V: THE SIERRA NEVADA

Several kinds of visits can be done. The shortest one goes across the low and medium mountain. The typical villages of the feet of the Sierra Nevada are located within 10 and 20 km, next to the most wooded area of the Natural Park, which has been already granted the rank of National Park. The headwaters and valleys of the Genil and its tributaries and the outskirts of villages like **Quéntar, Guéjar Sierra, Pinos Genil, Monachil, La Zubia**, etc. are interesting places. Vereda de la Estrella (lane of the star), the Quéntar Dam, Cachorros de Monachil (Monachil pups), Cumbres Verdes (green heights), El Purche, etc. are outstanding landscapes.
Its winter resort is an added attraction to the Sierra Nevada. It is called **Solynieve** (sun and snow) and is some 40 km far from Granada. It has different ski slopes for different kinds of skiers, ski lifts, hotels, nightclubs, all kinds of restaurants and many other services. The resort is located in the hamlet of **Pradollano** and there is a good road with plenty signposts that takes there and even further. Both for this excursion and the previous one, you can take a coach at the entrance of the Congress Centre or at the Ventorrillo Bar at the Paseo del Violón s/n. Compañía Bonal ✆ 958 273 100.

Outings in the surrounding areas

The crystal-clear waters of the river Dílar come down from the peaks of the Sierra Nevada.

The Sierra Nevada also offers opportunities for mountaineers. There are lanes and ways to get to El Trevenque, Loma de Dílar (the Hill of Dílar), the Veleta, the Alcazaba and the Mulhacén (3450 m). The landscapes are

Outings in the surrounding areas

stunning; both among the snow in winter, and in summer, when the ways are passable, despite there is also some snow in snowdrifts.

EXCURSION VI: ALPUJARRAS

The Sierra Nevada is a chain of mountains going from east to west. These peaks separate two shires in the east of the

Cástara, the quarter of the church.

province: the Alpujarra in the south and the high plateau of Guadix and Baza in the north. The **Alpujarras** occupy the southern skirt of the Sierra Nevada and part of the hills that spread to the coast. This is an area with unmatched landscapes, colourful villages and unique products. The traditional architecture is unique, with white walls, grey *launa* (crumbly type of clay found throughout the region) roofs called *terraos*, *tinaos* (bridge-like structures linking the houses), etc. There are dozens of villages scattered almost until the feet of the Mulhacén: **Lanjarón**, which is famous for its spring water and its health resort; **Capileira** and **Bubión**, hanging on the cliff; **Trévelez**, the highest village in Spain and famous for its cured ham; **Yegen**, where the British hispanist Gerard Brenan lived during the nineteen twenties; **Válor**, famous for giving its name to the ringleader of the *Morisco* rebellion; **Cástaras**, located in one of the most hidden and fresh rags; **Albodon**, famous for its wines; etc.

EXCURSION VII: THE HIGH PLATEAU

It is the shire located at the north of the Sierra Nevada. It is not as spectacular as the southern shire, but also very interesting for its near Castilian landscapes, its mining richness and its tourist attractions, many of them still not very exploited.

The most remarkable locality is **Guadix**. The main sight is the Cathedral, with its

Outings in the surrounding areas

Castillo de la Calahorra
(Castle of the Calahorra), south façade.

grandiose Baroque front and inside, similar to that of Granada. There is also a graceful main square, ancient palaces like Peñaflor, Gothic churches like Santiago and an Arab Alcazaba. The barrio de las cuevas (quarter of the caves) is also famous.

Near Guadix, there are **Purullena,** famous for its ceramics and troglodyte dwellings; **La Calahorra,** crowned with one of the best Renaissance castles in Spain; **La Peza,** placed in a lush valley and also crowned by the ruins of a castle; **Alquife** and its large iron mines; **Jeres de Marquesado,** a mountain village near lush chestnut groves that go up to the perennial snows; **Cortes** and **Graena,** with their busy health resort.

Heading north, a few mountains invade the high plateau, giving way to the Hoya de Baza. There, we find **Baza,** where the must visits are the Judeo-Arab baths, the Collegiate Church, the Alcazaba, a few mansions like that of Enríquez, some convents and the typical streets of the centre. Close to

Note

There is a comprehensive project for broad routes across Granada and its bordering provinces. It is the Legado Andalusí. The address of its information office in Granada is:

*Corral del Carbón.
C/ Mariana Pineda, s/n.*
✆ 958 225 995 / 902 195 195
FAX 958 228 644.

This tourism and cultural project is much more than the mere excursions around the surrounding areas of Granada. It offers predesigned long-distance routes, some of which get even to the north of Africa, and a wide bibliographic and audiovisual documentation about the survival and remains of ancient cultures that populated Andalusia.

Outings in the surrounding areas

Orce. Castillo de las siete torres (Castle of the 7 towers).

this locality, there is the **Natural Park of Sierra de Baza,** with all the charm of the mountains near Cazorla. Heading north again, there are interesting villages, like **Huéscar, Galera, Orce,** and **Castril,** most of which have ruins of fortress. Also worth visiting are the paleontological deposits in **Venta Micena** and the **Natural Park of Castril.**

EXCURSION VIII: THE COAST

The coast of Granada is not very extensive, but it is very diverse. The eastern landscape is rough, nearly wild. Deserted moon-like dry watercourses go down to hamlets like **La Rábita, Melicena, Los Yesos, La Mamola** and **Castell,** which have peaceful dark sand beaches. Going to the centre of the province, past a series of excellent cliffs for underwater fishing, we find the beaches of Calahonda, Carchuna, Torrenueva, Motril and

Outings in the surrounding areas

Salobreña. The tourist offer and the number of visitors gradually increase here. The western area is the most touristy, with **Almuñécar, La Herradura, Marina del Este,** etc. Here, the offer for sea sports, from sailing to scuba diving, is very wide, and there are also spots of ecological interest, like **Cerro Gordo.**

Dusk in the coast of Granada.

GRANADA IN A DAY
Basic itinerary

- If you have only one day to visit Granada, there are companies that offer minibus overview tours around Granada, and "The entire Granada in one day" tours. Two of them are:

Granavisión. ✆ 958 135 804
Dintur. ✆ 958 521 796

Morning

- Get the ticket to the Alhambra as soon as possible. The best way is ordering it in advance by fax or telephone.

- Spend the morning at the Alhambra, the Generalife and the adjoining museums. It is advisable to take a seat and rest from time to time, as it will be a long walking morning. There are fountains and plentiful shades here and there. There are also location signs and security staff that will kindly help lost visitors.

- Do not try to make a comprehensive visit. Go straight to the main sights *(Patio de los Arrayanes, Patio de los Leones, Partal,* etc.) and stop there for a few moments. It is better to get a general impression and the memories of a few areas than being overwhelmed by too much information.

- Have a peaceful lunch in any of the restaurants with views. If you still have the strength to continue the route during the rest of the day, the best option is a sandwich or fast food. However, a calm but not abundant lunch takes shorter than one may think, helps recovering strength and gives the impression of cutting the day in two halves.

- If it is possible, lunch and after-lunch should be done in the open air, which is a pleasant way to capture the Granadine atmosphere.

Afternoon

- The afternoon may be dedicated to the centre: Royal Chapel, Monastery of Saint Jerome, Cathedral and Cartuja. There will be enough time to visit the four monuments, allowing one hour for each monument and almost another for moving around.

- In the late afternoon –calculate the hour according to the time of the year– and after a fast snack to get strength back, walk up the streets of the Albaicin to see the sunset from any of its passages of San Miguel hill.

Evening

- The hurry-free evening must be saved for hanging about the Albaicin, enjoying its atmosphere, the *tapas,* the people… Then, walk down to the quarter of Pedro Antonio de Alarcón and enjoy the university nightlife.

- There are one thousand possible options: walk back to the Alhambra and admire the night lights, go to a concert at the Manuel de Falla Auditorium, walk around the gardens of the Huerta de San Vicente, where Lorca once lived, etc.

The surroundings of the Alhambra.

GRANADA IN A WEEKEND

FRIDAY

- If you arrive in late on Friday, use the rest of the day for a visit to the **Albaicin**. The Square of San Nicolás, with views to the illuminated **Alhambra** is a good option. Also, walk around the narrow streets of the quarter.

SATURDAY

- The **Alhambra** and the **Generalife** The earlier you go, the better. A full visit may take several hours. The sights in the area are the Alhambra Museum, the Gómez Moreno Museum, the romantic garden of the *Carmen de los Mártires,* Museum of Fine Arts, etc.

- It is always a good idea to have an aperitif at the **Plaza Nueva,** surrounded by its marry and pleasant atmosphere. The Elvira street and the *Paseo de los Tristes* are also excellent places for *tapas*.

- The **handicrafts shops** area is near the **Plaza Nueva** (Cuesta Gomérez). The Zacatín and the Alcaicería are also good for buying Granadine keepsakes, ceramics, etc.

- The afternoon may be spent visiting the **Cathedral,** the **Royal Chapel,** the **Monastery of Saint Jerome** and other adjoining churches.

- As well as its interest as a *Morisco* quarter, the **Albaicín** has important monuments opened to visitors, like the *bañuelo,* Santa Isabel la Real, etc. In the summertime, dinning in the open aire in a *carmen* with views to the Alhambra is always a good option.

- After dinner, going to the **Sacromonte** and attending to a *zambra* or flamenco show seems to be must. Still, there is also good flamenco in the Albaicin, at the Peña La Plateria. There are also dance shows in the Gardens of Neptuno, near the home of Federico García Lorca.

- The **movida** (nightlife) area for drinks and for joining the uncommon youth atmosphere is at **Pedro Antonio de Alarcón** Street. People stay up until the early hours.

SUNDAY

- If you choose to stay in Granada on Sunday, go to the **Cartuja** and then stop at the market of new and used items sited in the surrounding area (Almanjayar). An alternative for winter is going to the **abbey of the Sacromonte** and admiring the quarter on a sunny morning. Alter on, a good option is walking around the typical quarter of the Realejo and visiting its temples and then, at the aperitif time, going to the Campo del Príncipe for trying excellent *tapas* in a square with a distinctive charm.

- If you opt for a short excursion, you may choose among the **coast**, the **Alpujarra** or the **Sierra Nevada**. Any of them will take all day. In the first case, the best choice is going to Motril, Salobreña or Almuñécar, have lunch there and take a walk by the seaside. Hurries are not recommended for the Alpujarra: get to the rag of Poqueira and stroll around the labyrinths of the white little villages. If you would rather go to the Sierra Nevada, just follow the road to the Veleta and stop at the desired height. At some 2,000 m. of altitude, there is the ski resort (Pradollano), open and very busy during the winter.

- If you still have any strength left in the evening, you may go to a concert at the **Manuel de Falla Auditorium** or to some sporting event.

FESTIVITIES AND EVENTS
Festive events and other celebrations during the year

JANUARY
• **Fiesta de la toma (January 2)**. Commemoration of the anniversary of the entry of the Catholic Monarchs in Granada, on February 2 of 1492. The Mass in the Royal Chapel shines with its own light, with the banner hoisting from the town hall, and the cheering of the Granadine people.

FEBRUARY
Popular pilgrimage to the Sacromonte (February 1). Celebration honouring Saint Cecil, patron saint of Granada. There are regional dances in the open air, an excursion to the *siete cuestas* (seven slopes), a visit to the holy caves, picnic lunch, etc. ***Carnaval*** (Mardi Gras). Celebrations are mostly in Zaidín, Chana and other quarters. Both spontaneous and organized parades fill the lively streets of Granada with colour. **Delivery of the *Premios Andalucía* (February 28)**. Held at the Charles V Palace. These prizes honour those Andalusians who excelled at arts, creation, sports, investigation, etc.

MARCH
Saint John of God (March, 8). Co-patron of the city. Procession, sale of typical products, etc. **International Tango Festival**. The best figures of tango meet in Granada. Late gatherings at the bar La Tertulia. **Easter**. Famous and traditional religious processions. The most relevant brotherhoods are *El silencio* (the silence) along Acera de Darro, *Los gitanos* (the gypsies) on the way to the Sacromonte, *La Aurora* (the dawn) in the narrow streets of the Albaicin, *La canilla* in the Cathedral, Santa María de la Alhambra (Holy Mary of the Alhambra) in the Puerta de la Justicia, etc.

MAY
Día de la Cruz **(Day of the Cross, May 3)**. Celebrations in the entire city centre and the Albaicín, with *sevillanas* dancing and placing of crosses in different areas of the city. **Yearly polyphony meeting**. Held in Nigüelas, some 30 km from the capital. **Festival of Comical Theatre (middle May)**. *Casa de la Cultura* (Cultural Centre) of Santa Fe.

JUNE
Corpus Christi Fair and Celebration. Celebrated on the Thursday following the eight Sunday after Easter Sunday. It is the biggest fair in Granada and lasts for more than a week. **Bullfights**. Since the day of Saint Joseph, in March, until the celebration of the

Virgen del Pilar, in October, it is possible to attend to a bullfight, either *corridas* or *novilladas,* which are announced across the city in the traditional and attractive posters. As well as the essential bullfights of the Corpus Christy week, it is normal to have bullfights on the *Día de la Cruz* on May 3, on Easter Sunday, on the day of the Patron Virgin and in a few more occasions. **Popular celebrations and fiestas in the quarter of San Pedro (June 29).** A must go if traditional flavour lovers. **International Festival of Music and Dance (last week of June and first week of July).** One of the most prestigious in the world. Leading figures of the world of dance and music in the unparalleled background of the Alhambra and the Generalife.

JULY
Romantic concerts in courtyards and monuments (july-august). Special moments for the recreations of senses.

SEPTEMBER
Fiesta Rock of the Zaidín (middle September). One of the music events that calls a higher number of young people together, held in one of the most dynamic and modern quarters of the city. **Floral offering to the *Virgen de las Angustias* (September 15).** Another example of the roots of Granadine religiosity, surrounded by a background of colour and jolliness. **Feria general de muestras** (General Exhibit Fair). Held only in some years. **Celebrations in honour of the *Virgen de las Angustias* (last Sunday of September).** Patron Virgin of the city. In the afternoon, solemn procession of the image, embellished with all kinds of jewels; on the previous week, there is a autumn fruits market near the basilica. **Pilgrimage to the Hermitage of *San Miguel el Alto* (September 29).** Across the Albaicin, until the *Cerro del Aceituno,* where the hermitage is. Impressive views.

NOVEMBER
International Theatre Festival. Focused on creative vanguards. **International Jazz Festival.** Year after year, this event is taking a more and more relevant space in this intimist music style. **Santa Cecilia Music Week.** Held in the Higher Conservatory of Music.

DECEMBER
New Year's Eve at the Plaza del Carmen (December 31). This celebration follows the same tradition as many other Spanish cities, the perfect excuse for young Granadine people to party until New Year's morning.

INDEX OF NAMES

Albaicín	51
Albondón	134
Alcaicería	54
Alcalá la Real	125
Alcázar Genil	68
Alfacar	130
Alhama	125
Alhambra	37
Alhambra Museum	42
Almirante de Aragón Palace	66
Almuñécar	137
Alpujarras	134
Alquife	135
Antequeruela	65
Arab University	55
Arch of Elvira	52
Archbishop's Palace	60
Archive of the Chancellery	64
Atarfe	126
Baza	135
Bubión	134
Camino de Ronda	68
Campillo	64
Campo del Príncipe	66
Campo del Triunfo	70
Campus Cartuja Univ.	71
Capileira	134
Capuchinos Convent	71
Carmen de la Victoria	46
Carmen Rodríguez Acosta	43
Cármenes	51
Carrera de la Virgen	67
Cástaras	134
Castell	136
Castril	136
Castril house	45
Castril National Park	136
Cathedral	59
Cathedral Museum	60
Cerro Gordo	137
Cetti Meriem Palace	69
Colegiata del Salvador	52
Comares Palace	37
Comendadoras de Santiago Convent	66
Concepción Convent	45
Congress Palace	67
Córdoba Palace	46
Corral del Carbón	63
Cortes	135
Cristo del Silencio de Mora	54
Cuarto Real de Sto. Domingo	67
Cuesta de la Alhacaba	52
Chapiz house	46
Charles V Palace	41
Daralhorra Palace	53
Fine Arts Museum	42
Former Jesuit School	60
Former Mercedario Convent	70
Fuente del Avellano	46
Fuentevaqueros	128
Galera	135
García Lorca Museum-house	68
García Lorca Park	68
Girones house	67
Gómez Moreno Institute	44
Graena	135
Granada University	71
Guadix	134
Guéjar Sierra	131
Hermitage of Sacred Sepulchre	50
Hermitage of San Miguel	52
Hermitage of San Sebastián	68
Historic Archive	46
Hospitalicos	69
Huerta de Almanxarra	66
Huerta de San Vicente	74
Huéscar	135
Index of Names	144
Iznalloz	124
Jeres de Marquesado	135
Lanjarón	134
Loja	125
Madraza Palace	55
Manuel de Falla Center	44
Manuel de Falla Museum-house	65
Marina del Este	137
Melicena	136
Mezquita	54
Moclín	125
Monachil	131
Monastery of Sta. Cruz la Real	66
Monastery of Sta. Isabel la Real	53
Observatory of the Cartuja	72
Orce	135
Padre Suárez house	64
Park of the Sciences	68
Paseo de los Tristes	46
Perpetuo Socorro Church	61
Peso de la Harina	46
Pinos Genil	131
Pinos Puente	126
Piñar	124
Pisa house	44
Pradollano	131
Provincial Archaeological Museum	45
Puente del Rey Chico	46
Puerta de Elvira	69
Puerta de Fajalauza	52
Puerta de las Granadas	37
Puerta de las Pesas	53
Puerta Monaita	53
Purullena	135
Quarter of El Realejo	64
Quarter of San Matías	63
Quéntar	131
Real Monasterio de San Jerónimo	61
Royal Chancellery	44
Royal Chapel	58
Royal Hospital	71
Royal Nasrid Palace	37
Ruins of the Maristán	45
Ruins of the Puente del Cadí	45
Sacromonte Abbey	50
Sagrario Church	60
Saint John of God Basilica	63, 73
Saint John of God Hospital	62
San Andrés Church	69
San Bartolomé Church	52
San Cecilio Church	66
San Cristóbal Church	52
San Francisco Palace	43
San Ildefonso Church	70
San José Church	53
San Matías Church	63
San Miguel Bajo Church	53
San Nicolás Church	53
San Pedro and San Pablo Church	46
Santa Ana Church	44
Santa Catalina Convent	66
Santa Catalina de Zafra Convent	45
Santas Cuevas	51
Santo Domingo Church	66
Santos Justo y Pastor Church	61
Seminario de Maestros	46
Sierra de Baza National Park	135
Sierra de Huétor National Park	130
Sierra de la Alfaguara	130
Solynieve	131
Suspiro del Moro	128
The Alcazaba	52
The Bañuelo	44
The Calahorra	135
The Calderería	54
The Generalife	41
The Herradura	137
The Mamola	136
The Mill	74
The Peza	135
The Rábita	136
The Yesos	136
The Zubia	126, 131
Tiros house	64
Torres Bermejas	43
Trevélez	134
Valderrubio	128
Válor	134
Valparaíso	46
Vega de Granada	129
Virgen de las Angustias Basilica	67
Víznar	130
Yegen	134
Zacatín	54